DOWN ON THE FARM

*A Picture Treasury of Country Life
in America in the Good Old Days*

COMMENTARY BY

Stewart H. Holbrook

Pictures assembled and collated by Milton Rugoff

BONANZA BOOKS • *NEW YORK*

Acknowledgments

The author, picture editor and publisher gratefully acknowledge the help and suggestions of the following institutions, concerns and individuals in the assembling of the picture material for this book:

The Bettmann Archive, New York; Bostwick Studio, and particularly Homer Frohardt, Omaha; Brown Brothers, and particularly Harry Collins, New York; J. I. Case Co., and Fred A. Wirt, Racine; Chicago, Burlington & Quincy Railroad Co., and Val Kuska; Mrs. Karl D. Edwards, Colebrook, N. H.; Forth Worth Art Center, Forth Worth, Texas; F. Hal Higgins, Walnut Creek, California; Mrs. Myra Holbrook, Lemington, Vermont; Illinois Central Railroad Co.; The Library of Congress, and Miss Virginia Daiker and Milton Kaplan; Metropolitan Museum of Art, New York; The National Archives, Audio-Visual Records Branch; Nebraska State Historical Society, and Miss Myrtle D. Berry; the Newark, N. J., Museum; New York Public Library, and S. Ivor D. Avellino; New York Historical Association, Cooperstown, and Robert W. Crooks; the New-York Historical Society, New York, and Mrs. Bella C. Landauer, Sylvester Vigilante, and Arthur B. Carlson; Ohio State Archaeological and Historical Society; Oregon Historical Society, Portland; Office of the Postmaster General, Washington; Public Roads Administration, Washington; Roy E. Stryker, University of Pittsburgh; Superior Publishing Co., Seattle, and Ralph W. Andrews; Underwood & Underwood, New York; United States Department of Agriculture, Washington, and William J. Forsythe; Vermont Development Commission and Walter Hard, Jr.; Wisconsin State Department of Agriculture, Madison, and Cliff Hutchinson; State Historical Society of Wisconsin, Madison, and Alan E. Kent.

FOR

Bonnie & Tress McClintock

Table of Contents

DOWN ON THE FARM   9

A FARM WAS MANY THINGS   14

...and Many Moments   25

FINDING A PLACE...AND GETTING
    SETTLED   32

THERE WAS WORK APLENTY FOR A MAN   46

Fruit in Its Season   62

Services from Outside   70

AND A THOUSAND THINGS
FOR A WOMAN TO DO   74

AND ON THIS FARM HE HAD SOME
CHICKS, E-I-E-I-O   86

The Farmer's Best Friend Was His Horse   97

MACHINES MADE A DIFFERENCE   102

BUGGIES & SHAYS...FERRIES & SLEIGHS   114

SCHOOLDAYS, SCHOOLDAYS   128

   ...and Playtime   133

BUYING AND SELLING   142

OF FEASTS AND FAIRS AND
GET-TOGETHERS   156

   Sugaring Off   175

   Thanksgiving   183

Picture Credits are on page 188

Down on the Farm

IN THE EARLY DAYS of the Republic most Americans, like their fathers before them, were farmers. Those men in homespun who died on the smoke-hung green at Lexington were rustics, and so were those who stood at Concord Bridge. Among them they fired the shot heard round the world. Our first President was a farmer, and there could scarcely have been a member of our first Congress who had not turned a furrow, pitched a load of hay, or beaten a floor of buckwheat or rye with a flail.

That was the way nations were built. No one knew this better than Daniel Webster, a magnificent husbandman in his own right. "When tillage begins," said he in the sonorous periods of a native oracle, "other arts follow. The farmers are the founders of civilization." Webster had a right to say as much. While Secretary of State he built a plow with his own hands, a plow so mighty as to call for three yoke of stout oxen to pull it, while Secretary Webster himself held the share plumb in the furrow, urging his animals to greater efforts with bursts of expletive in Latin.

In those times some eighty-five per cent of our nation's workers were actually needed to feed themselves and the other fifteen per cent of the population. In the past century and a half this condition gradually changed, and today no more than fifteen per cent are required to feed *all* Americans, and meanwhile to export enormous amounts of farm produce and to pile up surpluses sufficient to create a considerable problem. During the past forty years alone our farm population has dropped from thirty-two to twenty-three million—which means that there has been a loss of nine million Americans from down on the farm.

"Down on the farm" is an American expression as firmly rooted as any we have. It refers to the place where most of our forebears, if not we ourselves were born. Because this is so, the phrase carries with it an image of times past. The picture may be dim or sharply defined, according to circumstances. To some it may conjure up old tales handed down for generations, of planting hills of corn in a forest clearing, with a flintlock leaning on a handy stump, ready for Indians. It may call to mind a jolly corn-husking, a sugaring-off, or the wonders of a state fair in posters plastered all over one side of a big red barn. It could bring memory of snow drifting down through shingles on the shed-chamber, to fall in little ridges on the crazy-quilt with the red squares. Or, it might be a truly splendid scene of fields standing full and golden with ripe grain, rippling over the horizon as a soft wind of early autumn brushed the tall stalks, and the man on the Deering reaper drove his team and day-dreamed that the yellow heads falling were double-eagles tumbling fresh from a United States mint. . . .

While the ordinary man merely remembered, his native poets celebrated life down on the farm in verse, his genre painters put it on canvas and wood and lithograph stone; and primitive photographers came along in a buggy carrying a monstrous camera to catch and hold the scene on tons of thick glass coated with silver chloride. The theater was not immune to the theme, and a farm-boy from Swanzey, New Hampshire, Denman Thompson, wrote *The Old Homestead,* then played it for thirty-three years on end, bringing mists to the eyes of hundreds of thousands of his fellow Americans whose memories retained the smell of a haymow in July, or the sound of a deep-toned bell on the neck of a graceful Jersey in the Back Forty.

The towns and cities of the United States today hold several million people who were born on farms, and millions more to whom the farm represents the life and times of their forebears. That is where the old homestead was, or is. This rural home and the life that went with it are still one of our great traditions. That both the home and the life have undergone an almost incredible change in the past half century is obvious to any observer. Improved machines are basic in the magic of the technology that permits fifteen farmers to produce incomparably more food than eighty-five of their grandfathers did.

The subject of this book of pictures is not the modern farm and farmer, but rather the farm and farmer of yesterday and the day before that, before machines and science transformed agriculture into factories in the field. This album is not, however, a lament for the past. It means to present a fairly representative panorama of the more or less Good Old Days of country life in the United States, and to let the individual imagination take over from there.

Being myself a farm boy, reared amid the fine scenery and on the stony difficult soil of Vermont, I know that the happy nostalgia which these pictures bring me is not exactly what the dictionary defines as "homesickness." The feeling, I believe, is more a wholly natural, if quite irrational sadness for one's lost youth. One's youth was spent, whether on farm or in the city, in a never-never land and time of marvels and joys and terrors beyond knowing. This pleasant mist of fiction through which most of us view our childhood will not in the least be dissipated by the pictures in this collection. Indeed, the pictures will more likely confirm the happy memories. Artists, after all, draw or paint no less with their emotions than with their eyes. And is there anyone who believes that a photograph cannot be subjective?

So, what you will see in this book is farm life as artists and photographers saw it. Many of them sought to picture the typical, the characteristic; others saw only the ideal. That is enough, too. The least of their works will touch a memory here and there, while the better of them may well set the imagination to calling up not only long-forgotten scenes, but the sweet sadness of remembered sound. I am sure that some of these artists thought they saw, even as you and I, a long meadow's waving grass fall beneath the cutter-bar of an old Buckeye mowing machine, as two stark white horses moved steadily through it; and the green timothy changed, as they watched, to amber hay; and soon to the door of the farmhouse, half a mile away, came your great-aunt or mine, conch shell in hand, to announce that the sun, or at least the Seth Thomas clock, had reached meridian and it was time for dinner. She blew into the shell, and it gave forth a trump that was heard across five farms, two brook valleys, and halfway up the mountain—a great, gusty, booming mellow note, deep and vibrant as the lowest note of an organ. It was a sound to arrest the stroke of a scythe in midair. When it died in echo, in the stifling heat of an August noon, the cicadas in the field resumed their farewell to summer, and to their youth. It is as beautifully melancholy a sound as can be heard in rural America.

Though that is a pleasant memory, and fitting to the place, some other farmboy might recall a wholly different and livelier scene, say in the flatlands along the Red River of the North, of one thousand acres of wheat in one field, and stretched across it the men of half a dozen threshing crews and six steam traction engines, vermilion collars around their stacks and billowing smoke straight up toward the sky, the biggest sky anywhere, a sky that reached from east to west, from north to south, leaving room for nothing else, save for a sun made copper by the haze of autumn. . . . Out there, in America's breadbasket, wheat growing on the stalk at seven in the morning was clean No. 1 Northern Spring by night—sacked, sewed, and rolling in a boxcar of Jim Hill's railroad to the flour mills beside the Falls of St. Anthony at Minneapolis. It was a scene of the husbandman's ultimate triumph over nature in the form of rain, drought, wind, frost, hail, grasshoppers, and rust. And it deserves remembering.

Yet, no matter what the scene, it has by one's middle years become idealized, a little hazy perhaps as to detail, but otherwise still fresh in the face of what Time has obviously done to everything else. Our memory is of a day when the world was young, the sky was blue and, despite its tribulations, the most wonderful place on earth was down on the farm. That is what the many pictures in this book are about. I can hope they will touch many a reader as they touched me.

Down on the Farm

A Farm Was Many Things...

SAVE FOR size, cities were much alike. But not farms. The very isolation of the farmer made for strong individuality. And in the vast sweep of America there were also the almost infinite differences of soil and climate. Three thousand miles lay between a potato farm in Aroostook County, Maine, and a stump ranch on the Olympic Peninsula of Washington. So did forty degrees of temperature and even more inches of rainfall. The cotton plantations of Georgia, centering around a mansion and the old slave quarters, reminded nobody of a 10,000-acre wheat ranch along the Red River of the North. The mellow clapboards of a pre-Revolution home in New Hampshire, where General John Stark had slept, were farther than mere miles from the sods piled to make a house and barn on the Nebraska frontier. A truck farm near New York City looked nothing like a Wisconsin dairy ranch, nothing like the covered fields of shade-grown tobacco in nearby Connecticut. Where a man found himself, he farmed according to soil and climate, and the market. Soil and climate even conjure up different gods. The Cape Cod farmer prayed for sun, he of Kansas for rain. Yet, whether it was New England, the South, the Midwest, or Out West, along the 100th Meridian, there were always remembered scenes that were dear to the heart of one's childhood. The scenes were as many and as varied as the people whose memories recall them. Time has faded some of them, but it has colored even more. Tucked away securely in memory, they have come to mean no less than *The Farm*.

The recollection could be of the sun breaking at last through the low-lying mist of early morning.

Or a barn, red against snow and gaunt trees, a well-used road curving to the milk-house. Or a white barn seen across an old rail fence between maples in full leaf.

*It might be the long shadows of tall elms beside a dirt road leading
to the house.*

It could be a tree-shaded, hilltop homestead in York State's Cherry Valley.

Or a cluster of houses and a windbreak standing out against the
wide Minnesota sky.

Or a Pennsylvania barnyard, with guinea hens and other such fowl
contemplating the arrival of their fodder for the season.

Or possibly a sod-house recently carved out of the rolling prairie.

Or, sod-house days forgotten, a Nebraska farmstead with a well-equipped barn, a new Adams windmill, a surrey in the carriage shed and lace curtains in the windows.

It might be a mere instant when the new mowing machine was about to take the field behind Star & Buck, with Grandpa, goadstick on his shoulder.

Or the white-pillared
dignity and serenity
of a plantation house
built in the great
days before The War

...or the spare,
sombre look of slave
quarters.

*It could be cows moving to the brook when the sun got high . . . or white
horses before a background of ripening corn and ready wheat.*

Or the classic well-sweep, as on Franklin Pierce's home in New Hampshire, designed to make the drawing of water easier for the women and children who usually fetched it.

Or the old mill-stream, with an overshot wheel like the one shown, or an undershot, to turn the great round stones that converted wheat into flour, corn into "Injun meal" . . .

Or the Village in springtime . . .

THE REMEMBERED scene would be an illuminated moment, a few seconds of time, which stands out fresh and vivid after many years — of a Red Cornish gamecock attacking a huge hawk that had swooped down to the barnyard, or of sighting a lost cow with calf among the mountain ash of the Back Forty. She who was a girl in a sunbonnet at the century's turn never forgot the instant when thick yellow cream began incredibly to pour from one spout of the shiny new DeLaval separator and pale skim milk from the other. It was magic. Sheer grace was watching her calicoed mother raise one arm and pull the perfectly balanced sweep to let a bucket down into the cool deeps of the farmhouse well. Her brother cherished a memory of a parade of Holsteins moving slowly through early morning mist from barn to pasture, and of ten acres of hayfield marked from railfence to stonefence with the rustic geometry of orderly windrows.

Water was where you found it, and there was that wonderfully serene moment on a midsummer's day when you let Dobbin cool his feet and drink his fill from the clear brook under the old log bridge.

And there was of course the old swimming hole, remembered as the painter Thomas Eakins remembered it in 1883, when he himself was thirty-nine.

Or sitting on the bars of the pasture gate, enjoying the world.

*Always there was the old storyteller who had perhaps served with Grant . . .
or maybe had merely killed a bear in the "good old days" . . .*

*"The old oaken bucket that hung in the well"
was another indelible memory . . . and the
sound of the crank . . . and the taste of the
clear cold liquid . . .*

*Or just watching Daddy emptying the sap
bucket into the tub.*

There were the dozens of times you picked daisies in the field near the old fruit trees.

Or the sight of a fearsome gobbler in full autumn panoply.

Or the period when a ride on the hayrick from barn to field was an exciting tour of the known world.

The flag is up, school's keeping, and horse and cutter are coming back after delivering their load of pupils to teacher.

Or, come Spring, when new colts no less than apple blossoms marked the season.

Then, there was that magic hour or so between supper and bedtime, when everything centered around the table and its Rochester Burner lamp.

Or the moment Old Mammy paused to have her picture taken with the latest as well as some of the earlier of her young charges.

Or proudly helping Daddy display the partridges shot for Sunday dinner in Vermont just across the upper Connecticut River from New Hampshire. (That's young Stewart Holbrook with his father.)

Finding a Place...and Getting Settled

THEY CAME from every state and from almost every country in Europe, and they were all moving with the sun. The West meant land, mostly free land. Land meant a living, perhaps even independence. The West did not stand still after 1800. In twenty years it moved from New York's Genesee Valley to Ohio. Another twenty and it was in Illinois, pushing against the Mississippi. Five years more and Iowa and Minnesota were being settled. In the Forties, too, began the classic if unexplainable migration across the Great American Desert by the route that went into history as the Oregon Trail. Thousands of families, bedeviled by all the elements, plus sand, mirage and Sioux, fought their way painfully every step over the bitter voids, then up and over one heart-breaking range after another, and down to the Pacific, even while the plains country behind them remained without one farmer and was still hunting-ground for buffalo.

By 1869 a railroad spanned the continent, and with it came a deluge of homesteaders, each to file, according to the Act of 1861, on 160 acres—Yankees, Southerners, Germans, Scandinavians, a few Finns and Belgians, and Hollanders, Poles, and Russians, tending mostly to follow their pioneer countrymen and settle in national groups. All had their problems. Those who chose the timber belt had to clear spruce or pine; those on the prairies must find water, find material for houses, barns, and fencing; and they could well expect trouble from Indians. The flatland farm was not complete until it had a well and windmill, a mile or so of barbed wire, and a Winchester rifle. The steady Western trek was marked by sudden land rushes, like the spectacular tide that swept into the newly opened Cherokee Strip, and the Bonanza Farm frenzy of the Dakotas. The Europeans were often better farmers than native Americans. They worked harder and they put in longer days. The next generation had a steam traction engine for plowing and harvest, and the one after that an all-purpose tractor and could scarcely speak or understand the language of its grandparents. Among them, the natives and immigrants homesteaded 248 million acres after 1861; and as long ago as 1890, the superintendent of the U. S. Census officially reported that the American frontier no longer existed. It had disappeared in less than a century. History had seen nothing else like it.

ILLINOIS CENTRAL RAILROAD COMPANY

OFFER FOR SALE

ONE MILLION ACRES OF SUPERIOR FARMING LANDS,

IN FARMS OF

40, 80 & 160 acres and upwards at from $8 to $12 per acre.

THESE LANDS ARE

NOT SURPASSED BY ANY IN THE WORLD.

THEY LIE ALONG

THE WHOLE LINE OF THE CENTRAL ILLINOIS RAILROAD,

For Sale on **LONG CREDIT, SHORT CREDIT** and for **CASH,** they are situated near **TOWNS, VILLAGES, SCHOOLS** and **CHURCHES.**

For all Purposes of Agriculture.

The lands offered for sale by the Illinois Central Railroad Company are equal to any in the world. A healthy climate, a rich soil, and railroads to convey to market the fullness of the earth—all combine to place in the hands of the enterprising workingman the means of independence.

Illinois.

Extending 380 miles from North to South, has all the diversity of climate to be found between Massachusetts and Virginia, and varieties of soil adapted to the products of New England and those of the Middle States. The black soil in the central portions of the State is the richest known, and produces the finest corn, wheat, sorghum and hay, which latter crop, during the past year, has been highly remunerative. The seeding of these prairie lands to tame grasses, for pasturage, offers to farmers with capital the most profitable results. The smaller prairies, interspersed with timber, in the more southern portion of the State, produce the best of winter wheat, tobacco, flax, hemp and fruit. The lands still further South are heavily timbered, and here the raising of fruit, tobacco, cotton and the manufacture of lumber yield large returns. The health of Illinois is hardly surpassed by any State in the Union.

Grain and Stock Raising.

In the list of corn and wheat producing States, Illinois stands pre-eminently first. Its advantages for raising cattle and hogs are too well known to require comment here. For sheep raising, the lands in every part of the State are well adapted, and Illinois can now boast of many of the largest flocks in the country. No branch in industry offers greater inducements for investment.

Hemp, Flax and Tobacco.

Hemp and flax can be produced of as good quality as any grown in Europe. Tobacco of the finest quality is raised upon lands purchased of this Company, and it promises to be one of the most important crops of the State. Cotton, too, is raised, to a considerable extent, in the southern portion. The making of sugar from the beet is receiving considerable attention, and experiments upon a large scale have been made during the past season. The cultivation of sorghum is rapidly increasing, and there are numerous indications that ere many years Illinois will produce a large surplus of sugar and molasses for exportation.

Fruit.

The central and southern parts of the State are peculiarly adapted to fruit raising; and peaches, pears and strawberries, together with early vegetables, are sent to Chicago, St. Louis and Cincinnati, as well as other markets, and always command a ready sale.

Coal and Minerals.

The immense coal deposits of Illinois are worked at different points near the Railroad, and the great resources of the State in iron, lead, zinc, limestone, potters' clay, &c., &c., as yet barely touched, will eventually be the source of great wealth.

To Actual Settlers

the inducements offered are so great that the Company has already sold 1,500,000 acres, and the sales during the past year have been to a larger number of purchasers than ever before. The advantages to a man of small means, settling in Illinois, where his children may grow up with all the benefits of education and the best of public schools, can hardly be over-estimated. No State in the Union is increasing more rapidly in population, which has trebled in ten years along the line of this Railroad.

PRICES AND TERMS OF PAYMENT.

The price of land varies from $7 to $12 and upward per acre, and they are sold on long credit, on short credit, or for cash. A deduction of *ten per cent.* from the long credit price is made to those who make a payment of one-fourth of the principal down, and the balance in one, two, and three years. A deduction of **twenty per cent.** is made to those who purchase for cash. Never before have greater inducements been offered to cash purchasers.

EXAMPLE.

Forty acres at $10 per acre on long credit, interest at six per cent., payable annually in advance; the principal in four, five, six, and seven years.

	INTEREST.	PRINCIPAL.			INTEREST.	PRINCIPAL.
Cash payment	$24.00		Or the same farm, on short credit:			
Payment in one year	24.00		Cash payment	$16.20	$80.00
" two years	24.00		Payment in one year	10.80	80.00
" three "	24.00		" two years	5.40	80.00
" four "	18.00	$100.00	" three "		80.00
" five "	12.00	100.00			
" six "	6.00	100.00			
" seven "		100.00			

The same farm may be purchased for $320 in cash.

Full information on all points, together with maps, showing the exact location of the lands, will be furnished on application in person or by letter to

LAND COMMISSIONER,

Illinois Central R. R. Co., Chicago, Ill.

PARADISE FOR SALE. *This poster is not selling the Garden of Eden but the next best thing—Western lands held by the Illinois Central Railroad Company. They could be had in the 1850's at $8 to $12 an acre, with 25% discount for cash. As a colonizer, the Illinois Central had few peers.*

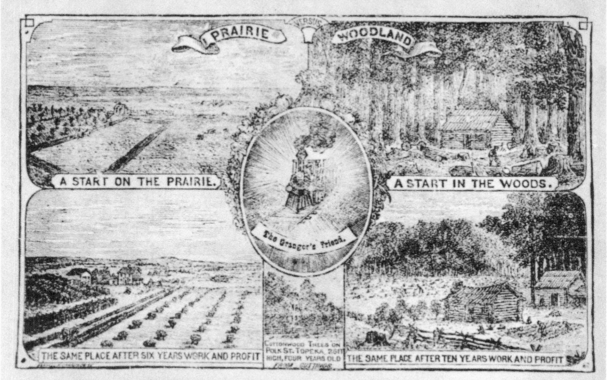

FREE LAND. *Farmers made new land productive, and the railroads (as above) did their best to lure them into the rush for claims. Most familiar of the pictures of a land rush shows frenzied claim-stakers plunging forward in wagons and on horseback into the Cherokee Strip on September 16, 1893. Below is a rare photograph of settlers on the Kansas state line who joined The Rush by Rock Island train.*

RELIC OF EPIC DAYS. *Six decades after the dust had settled along the Oregon Trail, a famous survivor, Ezra Meeker, retraced the route by driving an ox-team back across the plains.*

FACING A NEW WORLD. *To settle the American West, every country in Europe poured forth emigrants, like these freshly come from Belgium.*

ON THE WAY. *The new railroad took thousands of immigrants to the prairies; among them were a few artists, one of whom shows the Union Pacific's depot at Omaha as an exciting place filled with interesting people from everywhere.*

HOMESTEADING IN THE BIG TIMBER. *Homesteaders on the treeless prairies had work to do, and so did settlers in the Douglas Fir forest of the Pacific Northwest, where this remarkable photograph was taken by Darius Kinsey in the '90's. Clearing an acre in this wilderness of giant trees was an appalling job and the farms that resulted were understandably called stump-ranches. Not in some five hundred years before the Vanzer family came to homestead this spot had the sun penetrated to the forest floor. When the hardy picture-man called, the hard-working Vanzers already had a cabin, and a picket fence around the space for garden and orchard. Note young, newly-planted fruit trees.*

THEY CAME HARD. *If you wanted a field in Northern Wisconsin, you had to grub out the stumps, an exciting event when a Sampson puller was used.*

TREES HAD STOOD THICK. *There was one thing children reared on forest land never forgot, for these stumps might remain for generations.*

THE DAY THEY HIT WATER. *Water was one of the first things you had to have to make a home. When the well-drillers struck it on a prairie farm like this one, it was truly a great day, long to be remembered.*

THE PIONEERS. *Land cleared, well dug, house hewn out of the very earth itself, this sturdy farm family has given its answer to the cry, "Root hog or die."*

OUTBUILDINGS. *After the house and barn came the springhouse (top) to keep the milk cool, a cattle shelter (left above) of poles and hay, the ever-present outhouse (above), or a cowshed (left) next to the barn.*

GOOD NEIGHBORS. *Such a show as this Wisconsin barn-raising would not soon be forgotten by the young audience with grandstand seats. In early days a matter of necessity, it became a symbol of neighborliness and community spirit.*

THE FINISHING TOUCHES. *No barn was quite complete without the luck-piece over the door, the proud cock above the weather vane, or, in Pennsylvania Dutch country, the colorful pattern of the hex signs.*

GOOD FARMERS. *Good barns denoted good farmers. This New Jersey barn was a dandy, what with solid foundations, stone approach to the main floor, a sliding panel to permit easy use of the horse hayfork machinery, and at the top the lightning rods.*

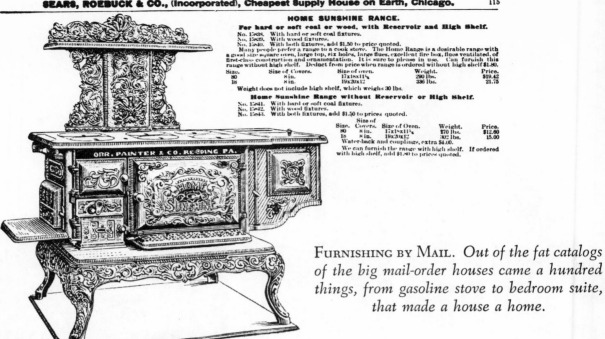

HOME SUNSHINE RANGE.

For hard or soft coal or wood, with Reservoir and High Shelf.

No. 15838. With hard or soft coal fixtures.
No. 15839. With wood fixtures.
No. 15840. With both fixtures, add $1.50 to price quoted.

Many people prefer a range to a cook stove. The Home Range is a desirable range with a good size square oven, large top, six holes, large flues, excellent fire box, flues ventilated, of first-class construction and ornamentation. It is sure to please in use. Can furnish this range without high shelf. Deduct from price when range is ordered without high shelf $1.80.

Size.	Size of Covers.	Size of oven.	Weight.	Price.
80	8 in.	17x18x11⅜	290 lbs.	$19.42
18	8 in.	19x20x12	336 lbs.	21.75

Weight does not include high shelf, which weighs 30 lbs.

Home Sunshine Range without Reservoir or High Shelf.

No. 15841. With hard or soft coal fixtures.
No. 15842. With wood fixtures.
No. 15843. With both fixtures, add $1.50 to prices quoted.

Size.	Covers.	Size of Oven.	Weight.	Price.
80	8 in.	17x18x11⅜	270 lbs.	$12.60
18	8 in.	19x20x12	302 lbs.	15.00

Water-back and couplings, extra $4.00.

We can furnish the range with high shelf. If ordered with high shelf, add $1.80 to prices quoted.

No. 15838.

FURNISHING BY MAIL. *Out of the fat catalogs of the big mail-order houses came a hundred things, from gasoline stove to bedroom suite, that made a house a home.*

SINGLE GENERATOR GASOLINE STOVES

1896 RELIABLE PROCESS.

Finest on earth. Greatly improved for 1896. These improvements to be found only in the Reliable.

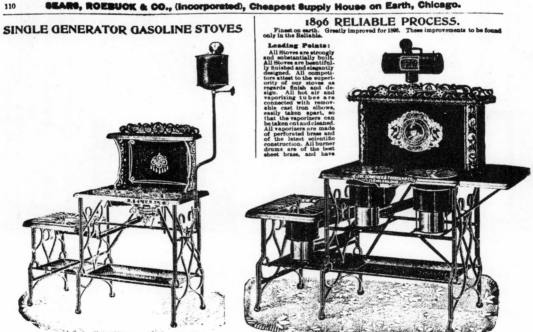

Leading Points:

All Stoves are strongly and substantially built. All Stoves are beautifully finished and elegantly designed. All competitors attest to the superiority of our stoves as regards finish and design. All hot air and vaporizing tubes are connected with removable cast iron elbows, easily taken apart, so that the vaporizers can be taken out and cleaned. All vaporizers are made of perforated brass and of the latest scientific construction. All burner drums are of the best sheet brass, and have

No. 15781. The **Reliable Single Generator Gasoline Stove, No. 22**, has two burners on top and one powerful double burner on step; a single generator serves all burners; every generator provided with a union joint coupling at bottom of stand pipe, and all generators have separate channels; size of main top, 20x27 inches; step top, 20x14 inches; high shelf, 7x22 inches; height to main top, 30 inches; height to top shelf, 44 inches; shipping weight, 106 lbs. **This is our leader** in this class of stoves, and is as strong, handsome and durable a stove as any one could wish. Price, with tin oven, $15.07; with Russia oven, $15.87.

Full directions for operating with each stove.

cast iron tops and bottoms. All cone seats are made of cast iron. All cone seats have large iron flanges so as to protect the drums from heat, grease and dirt, which have always caused burner drums to either burn or rust off at the top. This improvement makes all hot air conductors indestructible. A great improvement and one worthy of your consideration. All burners are fastened together with two bolts, easily taken apart. All tanks for 1896 are simple, perfect and a proven success. All needle points on valves are made of German silver wire; they will never rust or corrode, and will always insure a steady drip. All tanks are so constructed that they cannot be removed for filling until all valves have been closed. All Reliable Process Stoves will run perfectly in cold weather. All in all, the Reliable Process is the king of evaporating stoves.

The most beautiful stoves ever manufactured.

Our Furniture Department.

There is perhaps not another department represented in this catalogue where you will find more interesting bargains than in this furniture catalogue, and a careful comparison of prices and descriptions with those of any other concern will convince you of the great saving to be made by placing your orders in our hands. We believe we have a more complete furniture department than any other concern; in fact, want of space prevents our showing but a few of the most desirable goods in the different lines which we are able to offer you at special bargain prices, but for the accommodation of those who wish to learn more about our furniture and to aid them in making their selections, we

ISSUE A SPECIAL FURNITURE CATALOGUE,

the largest special furniture catalogue ever printed. It is a book 13x18½ inches in size and shows a most complete line of desirable furniture. The book will be mailed to any one free on application, although the postage alone is 7 cents, and we will deem it a mark of courtesy if you will inclose 7 cents when writing for this book.

Our line of furniture includes the products of some of the best factories in the country, in fact, we offer only strictly high grade goods, furniture made by concerns whose reputation is a guarantee for the quality of the same. We guarantee every piece of furniture to be exactly as represented, and if any piece or part wears out by ordinary wear in two years we will replace it free of charge. No other concern gives a like guarantee. If you place your order with us you are practically placing your order in the hands of the representative manufacturers of the land. We ship the goods to you at the manufacturers' prices, based on very large spot cash season contracts, with only our one small profit added, and on this basis you will own the goods at less than your local dealer can buy. The prices quoted are for the goods carefully packed, burlaped and delivered on board the cars in Chicago, and while you have the freight to pay, it will amount to next to nothing as compared with what you will save in price. Most furniture is accepted by the railroad companies at the regular first-class freight rate. We have given the shipping weight of the different pieces under the descriptions, and by referring to freight rates as explained in the front of the book you can calculate approximately what the freight will be to your place.

OUR SPECIAL TERMS ARE VERY LIBERAL.

We will send any furniture by freight C. O. D., subject to examination, on receipt of $5.00. You can examine the goods at the freight depot and if found perfectly satisfactory and exactly as represented, pay the freight agent the balance and freight charges and the goods are yours. If you send cash in full with your order we will allow you a discount of 3 per cent, and on quantity orders amounting to $60.00 and upwards there is a greater cash discount, as is fully explained in the front of this book. Nearly all our customers send cash in full. You take no risk, for if the goods are not perfectly satisfactory you can return them to us and we will cheerfully refund your money.

We are anxious for your first trial order, no matter how small, not for the little profit there is in it to us, but for the good it will do us as an advertisement. We will try to please you so well that you will willingly speak a kind word in our behalf to your friends, and in that way we will get more customers from your neighborhood. As we have often repeated, we have learned the best advertisement we can possibly have is a well satisfied customer, and we aim not only to satisfy every customer, but to treat every one at a distance exactly as we would like to be treated if we were in a customer's place; in short, treat every one alike, and that the very best we know how.

As an illustration of what can be saved by placing your orders in our hands and getting the manufacturers' lowest spot cash quantity prices, we offer you a

Complete Bedroom Suit, illustrated and fully described below, at $13.95, and on this particular bedroom suit we make you the following special offer terms: SEND US $3.00 as a guarantee of good faith, and we will send the suit to you by freight C. O. D., subject to examination. You can examine it at your freight depot, and if found perfectly satisfactory and exactly as represented, pay the agent the balance, $10.95, and freight charges, and the suit is yours. Or, if you send cash in full, $13.53 pays for the suit, and your money will be promptly refunded if you are not perfectly satisfied. We can offer you bedroom suits at even $5.00, or lower, but a really first-class article is always the cheapest, and if you can possibly afford to invest $13.95 in a suit we would recommend by all means that you order this one. You will find it equal to suits that retail at more than double the price. While you have the freight to pay, as before explained, it will amount to next to nothing as compared with what you will save in price. The suit packed ready for shipment weighs about 175 pounds, and the freight for 200 miles would be about 60c.; 400 miles, $1.00, etc., etc. From this you can closely approximate what the freight will be.

NO. 90—ORDER BY NUMBER.

Our artist has made the above drawing direct from this 3-piece suit. It has not been flattered in the least. On the contrary, no illustration we can show would do the suit justice. You must see it to appreciate it. The suit consists of 3 pieces, including 1 bed, 1 dresser and 1 commode.

THE DRESSER of this suit as illustrated in the picture is a very handsome one, being made like the entire suit, of solid oak, beautifully quarter sawed and finished to perfection. It is 5 feet 10 inches in height. It is decorated with very handsome hand carving, while the elegant mirror is made of the best imported bevel plate set in a fancy swing frame. The handsome double top of the dresser is 20x42 inches in size, and the dresser base is fitted with 3 very large roomy drawers with fancy cast brass handles. The baseboard is new style curved pattern, while the sides of the dresser are beautifully paneled and perfectly finished.

THE BED is 6 feet high, decorated with the same tasty hand carving as shown in the picture, and matches the decoration of the dresser exactly. The corner posts of the headboard are also ornamented with fancy carving. The top panel of headboard is also ornamented with fancy carving. The panels of both head and footboard are fitted to perfection, and the bed as a whole presents a most attractive appearance. It has a 4-foot 6-inch slat, and where mattresses, either wire or filled, are ordered with this bed, they should be 4 feet 4 inches wide and 6 feet long.

THE COMMODE is in every way strictly in accord with the general excellence of the suit. It is 5 feet high to the top of convenient splasher, has 2 roomy drawers with large two-doored compartment. These drawers have fancy cast brass handles to match those of the dresser. The sides are paneled and finished handsomely. The entire suit is fitted with very fine and strong patent casters.

45

There Was Work Aplenty

for a Man...

IT WAS ALL VERY WELL for the poet to sing that the farmer lived on the bounty of earth and led a life sweetened by the airs of heaven. What the poets blithely ignored was the labor required to make the earth give forth its bounty. A farmer's life was one of work, and more work. In spring came plowing, harrowing, planting, sowing. All summer he must weed, cultivate, fight pests. Then came haying, followed by the reaping and threshing of grain. There was no end to it: the old almanacs reminded him that December was the time to cut fuel for a year ahead, that January was for the ice harvest; in February he could cooper his sap-buckets and set his sugar-house in order; maple sugar time came in March, and if he did not have a sugar-bush, then he might well tend his fences, for April freed the sheep and cattle from the barn. By then, of course, he was spreading manure and plowing again. Always there was milking, night and morning; the care of animals, the repair of harness, wagons and equipment. He must saw his winter logs into stove wood, then split and pile it to season. If he needed a house, he built it himself; and so too the barn. Often he built his own dining table, the beds for his chambers, the chairs for kitchen and parlor. He steamed wood, bent it to the form of runners for his sleds, then covered them with shoes pounded from bar-iron. He could fashion a wheel with a hub of elm, the spokes of hickory. He was a competent butcher. He could lay a cedar-rail fence that would last a century, and a stone fence that would survive ten generations of his family—and still find them working early and late. That was the way it was with a farm and a farmer. He had the satisfaction of knowing that his labor was truly productive, that he was as much his own master as any man. And he felt with some reason that no other work was more important than his.

His work began before dawn with the barn chores. By sun-up, he was away to the fields.

The walking plow, with plodding, steady oxen leaning against their yoke was the favorite throughout the nineteenth century, especially in New England where this picture was taken in 1899.

SOWING.   Planting or "dropping" seed by hand (above) was as old as the hills. An endgate seeder (below) was a big step toward speeding up the age-old cycle. This was a favorite in many areas.

"Always there was the milking, night and morning . . ."

To get the welcome extra income of the monthly "creamery check," farmers brought their milk to the plant without which no rural community was complete. The sign by the small door of this creamery reads: "Sundays Milk to be Here at 6 A.M."

The universal or all-purpose farmer used his own wood for fuel and even for furniture. Oak or rock maple was best for burning. White birch was easiest to split. Yellow birch the hardest to split. Beech was a middling sort of wood.

LIFETIME JOB. *From the time he walked until he could walk no longer, every male on the farm had something useful to do.*

There was a Horatio Alger tradition on the farm, too. This good-looking lad of 1906 (above) became Governor Samuel R. McKelvie of Nebraska.

The older the man, the more likely was his scythe to be keen from the whetstone.

51

OLDTIMER. *The beard on this late Victorian is the so-called fringe type popularized by Horace Greeley, editor of* The New York Tribune *and notable friend of the farmer.*

WATER-BOY. *Given a gentle horse and a jug, youngsters on the great wheat ranches rode many miles daily to take something to drink to the harvest hands.*

For two centuries and more the American farmer cut grain with a cradle; and paused in the heat of the day for a swig of drink made of watered vinegar, a little sugar, a pinch of ginger.

MAN-OF-ALL-WORK. *When there wasn't enough manpower in the family, the farmer would hire the help. On most farms the Hired Man was an institution. Trying not to blink in the strong light, this one, a Vermonter at the turn of the century, has been keeping up with the farm world through the celebrated* Rural New Yorker.

JACK-OF-ALL-TRADES. *If the farmer himself didn't have the craft for all the thousand odd jobs around the farm, from mending a horse-collar to fixing a pump, he made sure he got a jack-of-all-trades hired man.*

Harvesting certain crops called for extra help, like this crew of pea-pickers
recruited from nearby villages. They were paid by the bushel and
usually lived in tent quarters.

Professional threshing crews often moved their machines by rail, following
the harvest from Texas to Saskatchewan.

PESTS AND PLAGUES. *The farmer was in a never-ending contest with nature. He couldn't do much about the wind and rain, or sun and sleet. But there were other enemies—birds and worms, borers and bugs—that he could fight. He could sheathe his cherries in cheese-cloth or his dates in brown paper. He could smoke out, poison, or shoot these marauders. Or he might simply scare them off.*

WHAT THE WELL-DRESSED SCARECROW WORE. *Were realistic scarecrows more effective than the simple ordinary ones? Many farmers thought so and kept the best cast-offs to drape the dummy in the corn field.*

DUCK & GOOSE POSSE. *In 1882 Dr. Hugh Glenn's California ranch was the biggest wheat farm on earth. Attracted by 45,000 acres of grain came thousands of ducks, geese and other birds, to be met by a posse of forty men who scared or killed the marauders day and night. Glenn figured this protection cost him some $30,000 a season, but saved him far more.*

NEW-MODEL PEST. *When the European corn-borer first appeared in Eastern United States around 1915, the only control seemed to be to burn infested stalks. This old-time New England farmer looks sadly at what in the spring had been a fine field of corn.*

ENTER THE SPRAYER. *The farmer's orchards were open country for all manner of diseases and voracious bugs. Forty years ago he began using horse-power dusters for protection.*

HORSE VS. WEEVIL. *Dusting cotton against boll-weevil with an old-time traction machine was slow, but much faster than by hand. This cart's wheels supplied power to operate the fan blast that blew the insecticide over the field.*

CATCHING CHICKEN FEED. *American farmers have been quick to invent gadgets to meet their problems. This hopper-dozer, pulled slowly over a field covered with the pests, caught them in the wire cage. Later they were dried for use as winter feed for poultry.*

GETTING READY FOR THE 'HOPPERS. *These ranchers of half a century ago are preparing for a grasshopper invasion of the stark Montana hills by mixing a bait of bran, molasses, lemon juice, water and crude arsenic. The best they could expect was partial control.*

Possibly for tradition's sake, this turn-of-the-century farmer is threshing out the grain on the barn floor by beating it with a flail, a tool dating from Biblical times.

When frost was on the pumpkin, it was time the corn was in the shock. That meant harvest days were over and winter could not be far off.

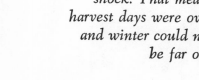

Generally known as "stoop-labor," picking potatoes by hand was hard work. Every September for half a century, whole trainloads of pickers were hired in Boston and shipped to the great Aroostook fields in northern Maine.

Diagonally across the land, in Fresno, California, grape growers cultivated their vineyards.

Fruit in Its Season

THE FIRST farm produce exported by American colonists was tobacco from Virginia. In years to come American farmers were to grow an endless number of crops for consumption at home and abroad. In time, Maine became known for potatoes, once grown chiefly for starch, but later for eating and for seed. Idaho came to dispute Maine, and even called attention to its tubers on its automobile license plates. Before the Breadbasket of the plains came into being, Ohio was so famous for its wheat that Minnesota flour was labeled "Muskingum," the name of an Ohio River. Indiana's great crop was corn. So was that of Illinois, Iowa, Nebraska. Wheat has led all or almost all in Minnesota, Kansas, the Dakotas, all over the Northwest, and in Oklahoma. From way back tobacco has been of first importance in the Carolinas, Kentucky, Virginia, Georgia, and Tennessee; and most of our cotton comes from Texas, California, Mississippi and Arkansas. In the past forty years sugar beets have grown into an immense crop, competing with cane. Vermont is perhaps best known for the product that comes from maple trees. Florida and California carry on an almost formal war over their respective citrus fruits. Washington boasts of its apples, Oregon is proud of its pears. They say the hens of no other state lay so many eggs as those of Iowa. There are more cows in Vermont than people, and Wisconsin makes a good portion of the nation's cheese.

APPLES. *Youth and age work side by side to grade and barrel the fruits of farm orchards.*

TOBACCO. Down South in the tobacco country the pleasant weed went into great sheds, there to hang in long leaves until dry and ready to bale for market.

COTTON. *In the cotton fields watch had to be kept on the new bolls to detect invasion of the almost certain weevils.*

BERRIES. *From Wisconsin.*

ONIONS. *From Texas.*

LETTUCE. *From Michigan.*

CLOVER. High in a mountain valley of Gallatin County, Montana, this 1927 crop of clover grown for seed brought the happy farmer a thumping $30,000, and his busy crew paused to have their picture taken for the paper.

PUMPKINS. *Giants, each one larger than the little girl and too big for so small a cart.*

MAPLE SUGAR. *Early spring brought the sugar harvest. The trees were tapped, buckets hung under the spouts, and then for three or four weeks the trunks poured forth sap that had to be gathered daily.*

HAY. *When sun and wind had made hay of cut grass, it was raked into tumbles, then pitched loose onto the rick, and away to the barn to the music of crickets, cicadas, and grunting oxen.*

ALFALFA. *A farm family poses proudly in front of a stack of bales.*

CHAMPION STACK. *In the cattle country of Eastern Oregon, hay was seldom put into the barn; it was baled, then piled into a mighty mountain like the one above.*

MAKING FARMERS' CHAMPAGNE. *The classic drink on many old-time farms was cider made from cull apples in late autumn. It was barreled fresh from a press such as this one-horse sweep-power mill, then stored in the farmhouse celler where, by late winter, it had developed a mild and happy condition called "hard."*

SYRUP THE OLD WAY. *This hardy old farmer is a traditionalist—boiling sap in an open kettle on an outdoor fire. To keep the thickening fluid from boiling over, he uses a piece of fat pork on the end of a stick—"pouring oil on troubled waters."*

Box Churn *Converting cream at a dairy in Kern County, California.*

"Grist for the Miller." *When he couldn't get a cash payment, the miller often took a portion of the meal.*

Sorghum. *Crushing the canestalks in an Ohio field.*

Services from Outside

ONCE A COMPLETELY self-sufficient community, the domain of the farmer gradually came to welcome services from outside. First among these, perhaps, were the physician on horseback with his medicines in saddle-bags; and the preacher in the form of the circuit rider, also ahorseback. Then, there was the blacksmith in the village or at the nearest four-corners-hamlet. The praises of all three have been the subject of legends and song. In former days, too, there was the itinerant tinker (his *dam* was a tool, not a curse), and the travelling shoemaker who lived with the family while he custom-made footgear ranging from copper-toed boots of cowhide to slippers of soft calfskin. There was also the drover who bought sheep, cattle, even pigs and turkeys, and drove them to market. In time, too, there came the postman with Rural Free Delivery, one of the greatest boons the farmer has known; letters, newspapers, and catalogs arrived, no matter the weather, at his individual post-office in the little box with the red flag at his very door. Later came the telephone that saved the farmer many a trip into town. And last but not least, there was the County Agent of the Department of Agriculture's extension service who, after a skeptical year or so, was found to be not a "professor" with doubtful book-learning but a friend bringing scientific help.

The County Agent ranged the rural districts giving welcome advice and valuable information. Shown here is Agent C. H. Hanson with his 1910 runabout.

Like many others, the farmer was at first skeptical of the telephone but soon found it a great time-saver and a friend in a crisis. And his wife discovered she could hear—and overhear—some very interesting tidbits of news on it. This one is a pre-World War I model.

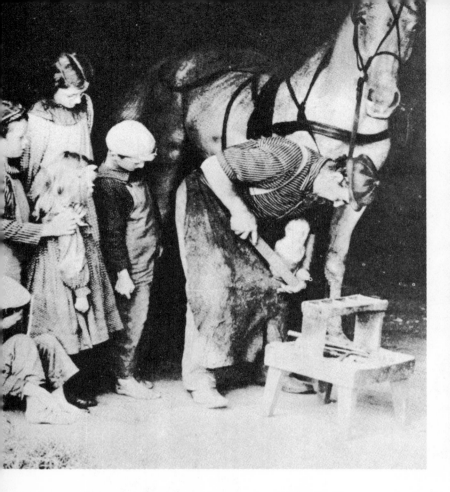

THE VILLAGE SMITH. *Though some farmers shod their own horses, the local blacksmith usually did the job. With his anvil, forge and hammers, he was an appealing figure, his shop a magic place.*

R.F.D. *Government touched the farmer in many ways, and none quite so welcome as in the Rural Free Delivery. This rig operated in 1899.*

BACHELORS OF CHEESE-MAKING. *By the century's turn, cheese had become so important in Wisconsin that the University added a course in the Swiss-type product at its Dairy School, of which these wonderfully moustached young men, posing with samples of their work and tools of their calling, were the first graduating class. Ought-seven was their year.*

And a Thousand Things for a

Woman to Do

HER DAY began before dawn, while it was yet dark. It usually did not end until the stars were out. She cooked for her household, which included a hired man or two, and often she cooked also for a multitude of hay-hands, balers and threshers. She made butter, tinting it yellow with the juice of dandelion root. She formed big round cheeses in a timbered cheese-press. When need was, she herself went to the fields to help with harvest. She picked berries and fruits to can. She made sausage. She smoked pork. She salted beef. In former times she made tallow-dips for light in the kitchen, candles for the parlor. The farm soap came from her grease kettle and wood ashes. In early days she washed and carded fleece, then spun it into yarn on a head-high wheel, walking to and fro, leaving a path in the rock-maple floor that could be seen a century later. She threaded the loom with her yarn and from it came homespun; or, she used flax for the warp, wool for the weft, and wove linsey-woolsey. Then she made clothing. Quilts, mittens, socks, needlepoint and lace, these were among her arts and crafts; and so was the delicate sampler with the motto from Whittier: *The Hope of All Who Suffer, the Dread of All Who Wrong.* She gathered herbs which she hung to dry in the shed-chamber, and with them cured the family ills. She was midwife. She was nurse. And at last she dressed the dead for their coffins. She was only too often taken for granted, but in the West at least, where she often defended her home with a rifle, she stands in bronze in many a park as the Pioneer Mother.

The food department included a lot more than cooking. There was baking and canning, preserving, taking care of the root cellar, making cheese, butter, candy, ice cream, and all the rest.

DISHWASHING. She was held a lucky woman if the house had running water and taps.

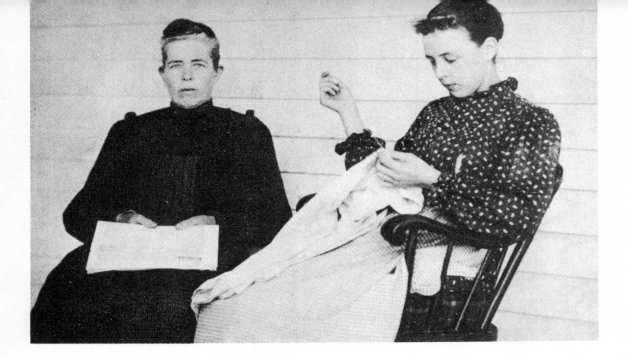

SEWING. *You could "send away" for almost everything or buy it in "the store." But the good housewife bought her calico, muslin or other yard goods and sewed it herself.*

WASHING. *This was hardly a chore to be proud of, but when the man came "to take a picture," everyone wanted to be in it.*

What she called her Busy Work covered the field—quilts, mittens, socks, samplers, even lace.

For festive occasions, she got out the sturdy White Mountain Freezer to make ice cream such as no store ever knew.

You could put fruit down, you could put it up, it was all the same and it went into Mason jars, as in this farm kitchen equipped with a hand pump.

Cookery with a fireplace called for special skills. Before pies went into the Dutch oven, a fire was built in it and, when hot enough, the ashes were raked out. Meat was commonly roasted on a spit over the open fire, but this cook is using a metal reflector to cook the spitted goose inside. Kitchen fireplaces began to disappear when cookstoves were introduced in the first quarter of the last century.

Sometimes it was a welcome change to go outdoors for water from the well,
or a jar of preserves from the outdoor cave.

In former times, she saved the kitchen grease, added potash, and made both
soft and hard soap in a big black kettle.

Often enough, the farm wife made a little pin money by selling fresh apple cider from a stand at the edge of the orchard. Or it might be eggs, corn, berries, tomatoes, apples or whatever.

Alongside an adobe hut in Texas a well-groomed woman, riding sidesaddle, guides a barley-laden donkey back from the fields.

And sometimes, when there was no other help to be had, the farmer's wife chipped in and did real farmer's work—sawing wood, picking fruit and calling the cows. The woman shown at the right, below, won a calling championship in which most of the entrants were men.

REMEMBER THE FARMERETTES? *During the
labor shortage in the first World War, women
and girls of all ages got into bloomers and
smocks and trooped into the fields and
orchards as the Farmerette Army. They even
drilled by squads, as in this picture of 1917.*

AGENT IN THE MOUNTAINS. *This dedicated
young woman, a home demonstration agent of
the U. S. Department of Agriculture, covered
her route in the Kentucky hills on horseback.
The box carried all equipment needed for her
work, dealing with the proper preservation of
foods, sewing and other domestic activities.*

Somehow there was always time, after the chores were done, for a woman to pore over the wonderful bargains so elegantly pictured in the latest issues of the mail-order catalogs.

MILLINERY DEPARTMENT—(Continued).

No. 2942.

No. 2942. Young ladies' dress hat, black Canton braid fancy edge. Trimmed with wide all silk satin ribbon, fine chantilly lace, gilt stick pins and fine French flowers..................$2.75

No. 2944.

No. 2944. Another novelty in dress hats. Made with tape crown and fancy rim, handsomely trimmed with fancy Chantilly lace, loops of wide all-silk satin ribbon, pretty buckle and elegant French roses. Color, black only.
Price $3.50

No. 2943. Fine Russian hair braid, with straw cord edge, in black only, trimmed with wide all silk satin ribbon loops, cut steel stick pins and fine French flowers and foliage.
Price $4.50

No. 2946. Young Ladies' Face Hat, in black only, made of fine Russian hair braid. Trimmed with wide loops of satin ribbon, jet stick pins and fine apple blossoms, Chantilly lace under rim. This is a very rich and dressy hat, copy of a $5 imported pattern. Our price......$4.50

No. 2945.

No. 2945. Fine Canton, with fancy edge, in black only; trimmed with extra wide all silk satin ribbon, bows and puffs around the crown, fine jet buckle and imported rubber stem roses.
Price..................$2.50

No. 2943.

We send any Hat C. O. D., subject to examination, on the most liberal terms.

No. 2946.

All our hats are direct copies from the finest patterns imported from Paris.

No. 2949 is a regular $10.00 Hat for only $4.00.

No. 2947.

No. 2947. Open fancy lace braid trimmed with loops of Chantilly lace. Jet stick pins and fine French flowers. Color; Black only. This is a good sensible hat and very dressy..................$2.25

No. 2948. This beautiful hat artistically trimmed with wide all-silk satin ribbon, loops of straw cord and exquisite French roses and buds, and fine gilt buckle. The hat is black, fine tape crown, fancy plaited rim, fine Chantilly lace under rim. Colors; Black only..................$4.00

No. 2949. Fine White Leghorn Flat, turned up back and side, trimmed with wide all-silk satin ribbon plaits around the crown and under rim; beautiful fine French flowers and foliage. This hat is a modified copy of a pattern costing us $10 to import.
Our price..................$4.00

No. 2948.

No. 2949.

The New Marlborough Collar for 75 Cents.

No. 21284. The latest creations in novelties, made of very fine dotted Swiss, Irish point embroidery edge, with the new Venise double edge inserting bands, prettiest open work imported and will launder handsomely. Postage, 5 cents. Our special price. **$0.75**

Our 79 Cent Fancy Collar.

No. 21286. Ladies' Fancy Collarette with fine satin collar and two satin points. Full 10 inch Point de Ireland Lace edge, of handsome butter color. Our stock includes only the latest styles for 1896 and none is more suited to the popular taste than the elegant lace collar shown in the illustration. If not satisfactory any purchaser may return the goods and we will promptly refund money. Postage, 5 cents.

No. 21289. One of these elegant Collarettes in a neighborhood at our special wholesale price will sell to everybody else who sees it. We have taken the entire stock of the manufacturers at rock bottom figures and sell at actual cost of the same goods to the retailer.

The special sample shown in the illustration is the late style of Marlborough yoke collar made of fine velvet, very wide butter color Point Venise or Pleauon lace 8 inches deep, collar is also trimmed with two rows of Valenciennes lace to match border. Our special price leads us to prophesy that we won't

have one of these collars left in six weeks. Better send in your order at once and be sure of getting one of these $2.50 Collarettes at our special price. **$1.25** Postage, 8 cents.

A Gem for 85 Cents.

No. 21287.

No. 21287. Made of Moire silk in bands and points in any color, very full reveres and edging of the new Point de Paris lace. This particular collar is all the rage in this city. Our special price, each. **$0.85** Postage, 5 cents.

A $2.50 Collarette for $1.60.

No. 21290. A picture or printed description **cannot do this elegant Chiffon collarette** half justice. You must see and wear it to get a fair idea of its beauty. One of the latest and swellest pieces of neckwear on the market. Strictly latest style for 1896; made of very fine Chiffon lace, with six **ornaments** of **Point Venise or Pleauon lace**, as shown in the picture. High collar of Chiffon, lined with French crepe; a decided hit of the season; guaranteed satisfactory and a great bargain or money refunded. Postage, 6 cents. Our special price, as a spring trade starter. **$1.60**

Our $1.95 Beauty.

No. 21291. Beauty and quality are combined to a remarkable degree in the elegant collarette illustrated. Made of very fine Habutai silk, ornamented with alternating rows of shirred silk and **Point Venise Insertion**; very wide lace border all around. Silk comes in popular shades such as cardinal, light blue and pink. A very showy collar that will add effect to any dress. Our price makes it possible for poor as well as rich to dress handsomely and in the latest style. Retail price, from $2.75 up. Postage, 6 cents.

Ladies' New Style Neckwear.

Made extra long to tuck in belt; guaranteed the latest styles for season of 1896. If you give us your order you will be sure to get the very latest high art goods. No seconds, no last year's stock, no old styles. Our Liberal Terms of C. O. D. on receipt of $1.00 prevails throughout this line as well as our entire Furnishing Goods Department. Many of these goods can be sent by mail at a very small expense; always inclose enough extra to pay postage. Remember our 3 per cent. cash discount. Allow about 3 cents postage for a tie, 6 ties in one package, 12 cents postage.

No. 21292.

No. 21292. Teck Scarfs for Ladies, prettiest, newest effects, light or medium shades. Each. **$0.12½**

No. 21293. Ladies' handsome Satin Teck Scarfs, extra long to tuck in belt. Colors; cardinal, navy or black, not figured. Each. **$0.20**

No. 21294. Ladies' extra long Silk Teck Scarfs; new select fancy checks, stripes or figures, light or medium colors. Each. **$0.25**

No. 21295. Teck Scarfs; made with a shield (without band) for turn-down collar only, handsome silk check or figures, medium color. Each. **$0.25**

No. 21296. Beautiful quality figured Jacquard Satin Teck Scarfs, white or colored ground and small colored figures; handsome new effects, satin lined, tailor made with band to go around the neck, can be worn with standing or turn-down collar. Each. **$0.45**

Ladies' Four-in-Hand Scarfs.

No. 21298.

No. 21297. Ladies' Fine Japanese silk scarfs in handsome light colors and tints, pretty figures and watered effects, length, 48 in. Each. **$0.18**

No. 21298. Newest and prettiest brocade silk effect in beautiful light colors, pearl, lilac, robin's egg blue and other pretty shades; length, 48 in. Each. **$0.20**

No. 21299. Rich Persian effects is a very swell and handsome four-in-hand scarf, 48 in. long, made of fine silk, satin lined, light and medium colors, this is the latest novelty shown. Each. **$0.45**

Windsor Ties.

Fine quality and large assortment at manufacturer's prices. New select patterns for Spring and Summer of 1896. Neat pin stripes, pencil stripes, checks, new effects in Scotch plaids, also handsome dainty fine figures and new Persian effects, in fact we have any desirable style and expect a very large trade in this line because Windsors will be very much worn by gentlemen, by ladies and by the children. We have ties to suit all, any color or combination required. It would be a capital idea when ordering a shirt or shirt waist to order a tie that will harmonize in color, you will be sure to get something to please you and look well, the following are some specialty good numbers:

Allow 2 cents postage for Windsor ties.

No. 21300. Handsome neat pin stripes, fine sateen Windsor ties, looks like a silk in different colored ground, pink, lilac or light blue. Each. **$0.04** Per doz. **0.40**

No. 21301. Fine checks, the same as above. Each. **$0.04** Per doz. **0 40**

No. 21302. Handsome Black Lace Striped Windsor Ties, with a group of small satin stripes between each lace stripe, very pretty and looks like a half dollar tie. Our price each. **$0.07** Per doz. **0.75**

100-pound orders economize freight. Add groceries or hardware to make 100 pounds.

When you build your house you will need Hardware, Doors, Sash, Blinds, Paper, Roofing, Paint, Etc. We will save you 35% per cent. When you furnish your house you will need Beds, Tables, Dressers, Couches, Carpets, Draperies, Stoves, Etc. We will save you 35% per cent. Get prices from Catalogue or write for complete estimate.

UNEXCELLED LACE NARROW SQUARE TOE.

No. 324. This shoe is made from the finest vici kid, is hand turned, narrow square toe, with imported patent calf tip, medium weight sole, new scroll heel foxing, double stitched, fine patent leather lace stays up front, and a handsomely trimmed top. We anticipate a very large sale on this shoe, and we guarantee it to be equal in style, fit and wearing qualities to any shoe sold at double our prices. Sizes, 2½ to 7; widths, A, B, C, D, E and EE. Per pair, $2.65.

SOLID COMFORT.

No. 325. This shoe is made from good dongola stock, low heel, broad toe, soft and pliable sole, and we guarantee it to be as easy as any shoe ever sold. This shoe is always in style and suitable for young or old. Sizes, 2½ to 8; widths, E and EE; weight, 25 oz. Per pair, $1.73.

LADIES' SQUARE TOE BUTTON.

No. 326. This shoe is designed for those who can not wear the needle toe last and still wish a neat appearing shoe. It is made from a good grade dongola, medium heel, and square toe with patent leather tip. Sizes, 2½ to 8; widths, D, E and EE; weight, 20 oz. Per pair, $1.65.

SHREWD BUYERS

Always look for the best of it. The man who wants to become comfortably fixed financially, and lay up something for a rainy day, doesn't pay $2.50 for a pair of shoes when he can get the same value elsewhere for $1.69. He doesn't pay his local dealer $80 for a Columbus top buggy that Sears, Roebuck & Co. sells for $39.90.

He has our Catalogue on his table, and it saves for him the dealer's profit.

liberal if you want to have goods sent

No. 58. Extra fine Cambric Laundered Waists, with detachable collar and attached cuffs. A very sensible garment. Made of Spring Brook Cambric, fast colors, white ground, with blue, pink or black pin stripe and dot, with gathered front, double pointed yoke back, dress-maker made. Each $1.25

No. 2546. Exposition, perfectly shaped and a fine fitting corset, equal to any retailed at 80 cents; made of heavy jean, stripped with sateen, wide zone, double busk, two side steels. Colors; white, drab, cream or gold. $0.40

No. 2547.

No. 2547. Best quality jeans corset, striped with sateen, bone bust, two side steels, 6 hook clasp, embroidered at top and bottom, in shape, appearance and durability equal to any $1.00 corset; unquestionably the best corset ever produced for the money we ask. Colors; white, drab or black. $0.50

No. 2549.

No. 2549. This corset is modeled after the finest French shapes and will fit any lady of average proportion; it is made with soft busts and stayed with unbreakable French wire. Colors; black or drab. Size, 18 to 30. $0.75

No. 2550.

No. 2550. French Contel Corset; extra long waisted; sateen stripped; fitted with unbreakable French wire; trimmed with handsome silk embroidery and heavily flossed, and produces an elegant appearance equaled only by corsets costing double the money. Colors; White, drab or black. $0.95 Extra size in black only, sizes 31 to 36. $1.25

No. 2554. Comfort elegance; a summer corset; made of imported netting; stripped with satin; reinforced steels, two side steels, and extra heavy back wire; six clasp; as perfectly fitting as any of the higher price corsets. Colors, white or drab; sizes 30. $0.

No. 2554.

No. 2555. A well summer corset, double busk; two steels; wide zone; white only; sizes 18 Price $

No. 2556. Nursing Corset. The most sensible convenient and comfortable nursing corset made; well staid on the sides, but very pliable over the sensitive parts of the body; the opening permits the use of nipple without the least inconvenience; made of fine jean. Colors; White or drab; size, 18 to 30. $0.90

No. 2556.

Dr. Warner's Coraline Corset

No. 2557. Made in medium length; well adapted to ladies of average figure. This set has been before the public for fifteen years, has the largest sale, gives the best service of any corset ever manufactured. Made in two thicknesses of fine corset; heavily boned with coraline in a manner that prevents the corset losing its shape, makes it absolutely unbreakable. Hip is extra wide with cluck spring side steels. Colors, white or black. Each $. Extra large sizes, 30, 35 cents extra.

No. 2557.

84

And always there was the latest occupant of the baby buggy. The clapboard siding might go unpainted but Baby's carriage was fit for a prince.

And on This Farm

He Had Some Chicks, E-I-E-I-O

TO SUMMER visitors from the city, the farm was like a menagerie. Roosters waked them. Cowbells in pasture tinkled through the afternoons. Nights brought soft, sleepy mooing from the barn. By day, guinea fowl screamed, gobblers strutted and scolded, common hens called attention to eggs just laid. Ducks and geese carried on interminable conversations. There was the occasional bellow from the ringed bull and the bleating of his many children. Sheep pleaded gently. Pigs grunted contentment. Horses whinnied for provender. And above everything else, now and again, was the astonishing noise of a healthy mule in full bray. To the farmer all these sounds were casual and commonplace. His barnyard was the Peaceable Kingdom where the lion lay down with the lamb—or almost. His animals provided him with food, often with clothing, always with motive power. The good farmer took excellent care of his animals, housing them well, treating them with all manner of medicines when they were ailing, and offering handsome rewards for their return when they were lost, strayed or stolen. Farm children were never without pets. Favorites were cosset lambs. Calves were permitted to suck one's finger and were generally babied until nearly grown. Barn cats were taught to sit up and catch milk squirted from a cow's udder. Breaking colts was fun, and breaking young steers to the yoke was almost like being an old-time ox-teamster. There was always a dog—usually a Scotch collie with an inherent ability to herd cows. In wooded regions, a motherless fawn often followed cattle to the barn, and so became a pet. But others were harder to tame: baby partridges seldom thrived in a pen; and a bear cub, for all his clowning, was never to be trusted.

Feeding the barnyard fowl was, often enough, a boy's first responsibility.

"A duck, duck here, and a duck, duck there . . ."

"Cosseted . . . and made much of," wrote Oliver Wendell Holmes, using a word which on the farm was applied to a cosset lamb, one bereft of its mother and reared on bottle milk.

Even a nanny goat could attract a youngster's fancy.

And a young colt could win anyone's heart.

POSING THE PETS. The farm child without a favorite animal was rare. The two younger pet owners shown here knew how to soothe a lamb and a calf by holding a finger in the mouth of the animals.

BLAZE. With his fine full-length blaze, this young girl could probably spot her horse a mile away.

If there weren't too many cows, you had names for them and made friends with them, and they with you. Toward evening they'd come close to the house and crowd the wash-lines, waiting for you to come and milk them.

"How do you like that?" this cow, suckled by piglets, seems to be saying.

WHEN A COW WAS A COW. *In the days before Bossie was a mechanically operated milk-machine.*

A CALF IS BORN. *Alone in the pasture this cow gives her new-born baby a "sponge bath" with her tongue. After that Baby tries to stand, finally succeeds, and wins its first meal—all the milk it can drink.*

Bulls were notoriously uncertain of temper; hence the ring in the nose of this fine registered Guernsey of Hinsdale, Illinois. Anything red was supposed to anger them, and farm women a-berrying in the pasture were careful to avoid that color in clothes. Many farmers have fallen victim to their own animals.

This registered Ayrshire bull shows a fine pair of horns. He was "dropped" in 1904, but if it were 1940, the horns would have been cut off very early in his life.

Pigs Is Pigs. *No farm animal multiplies faster than pigs. A litter averages seven. Ten are fairly common. A record was nineteen. Yet many a farm-boy who planned to get rich with hogs soon found that they were prone to many diseases.*

THE SHORN LAMB. *With a good nine pounds of wool removed, a shorn sheep looks forlorn next to one in full fleece.*

BRANDING TIME. *Unlike cattle brands, sheep brands are not burned in but applied to newly sheared animals with a stain that holds its color in the new wool for a year to come. Brands are registered with the state.*

Even if Nature couldn't, Harvell's powders would.

WHITE MULE. *You couldn't ever be really fond of a cantankerous, blankety blank animal like this, but you had to respect him for his strength, his independence and of course his kick.*

MULE TRAIN IN THE WHEAT. *Some farmers believed mules had more stamina than horses, and one wheat grower of Eastern Washington preferred this 20-mule team for the killing job of hauling a big combine that cut and threshed in one operation.*

The Farmer's Best Friend Was His Horse

THE OX WAS the American farmer's first work animal. Though he was soon largely supplanted by the horse, or mule, his great calm and his steady if slow gait have kept him from complete extinction. But for more than two centuries the horse stood alone as the farmer's beast of all work, with the mule close behind. Even the appearance on the farm, in the late 1870's, of steam traction engines did not displace the horse. He continued to thrive for decades, for both horsepower and steam-power units grew steadily in numbers until World War I, when the gasoline tractor started to displace them. As late as 1915 there were nearly 27,000,000 horses and mules on American farms. This was at or near the peak. Forty years later the number had dropped to six million.

A man knew every spot, dot and blemish of his horse and his harness.

$50 REWARD

Stolen from the barn of the subscriber, on the night of October 19th, 1883, one Chestnut Horse, weight about 1,000 lbs., heavy black mane and tail, with white stripe in forehead; also, one single Buggy Wagon, painted black, booted behind, both shafts having been broken and mended; one old single breasted driving Harness, both tugs having been broken and mended; two old Blankets, and a Valise with two locks.

Fifty dollars reward is hereby offered for the return of the property, or the arrest and conviction of the thieves.

ARAD JACKSON.

Barre, Vt., October 20th, 1883.

A good master was a workhorse's only reward.

SHOO FLY. *A good inventor is equal to anything, as witness this four-piece suit which was supposed to free Dobbin from stable flies, blue-bottles, horse and deer flies, mosquitoes, or any other insect given to troubling horses.*

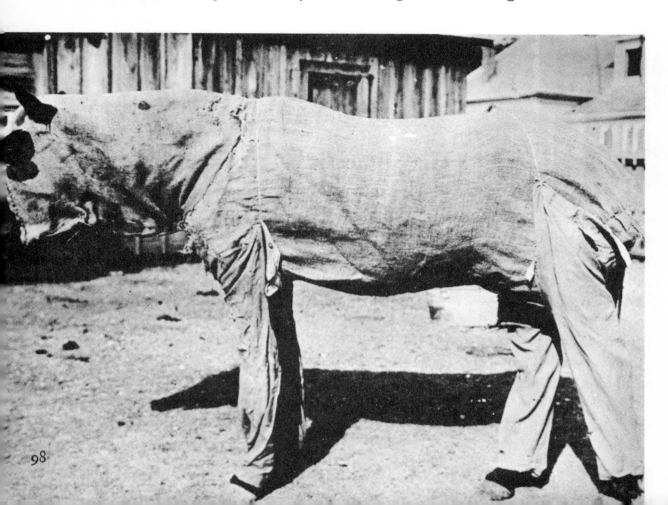

THEY WENT ROUND AND ROUND. *With a sweep-power, the driver took his place in the center, like a ringmaster, and talked constantly to his animals, offering praise and blame, and, if need be, touching them lightly with the whip. The teams usually spelled off after two hours or so.*

SULKIES, TROTTERS AND PACERS. *A man could be proud of his fast Standard-Bred horse, who might not always win at the county fair races, but could beat any other horse in an impromptu match on a country road.*

165 LIVE HORSE-POWER. *For many years a favorite picture-postcard mailed Back East by the hundreds of thousands, this scene on the Drumheller ranch near Walla Walla, Washington, shows 165 head of horses hauling five combines, all in one field.*

In effect, a detail of the above combination, except for one row less of horses.

When this Winton Six touring car appeared on the road in 1903, it marked
the beginning of the end of an era.

Wistfully the horse looks at the rattling tinny contraption that is destined to
end his major role on the American farm.

Machines Made a Difference

WHEN THE nineteenth century opened, the American farmer was working with almost the same equipment his remote ancestors had used in Europe. Indeed, the cradle was perhaps his only "modern" tool. Yet by 1850 a horse-powered mowing machine had started to replace the scythe, a reaping machine was cutting grain, a threshing machine was replacing the flail. By 1870, steam was doing some of the plowing, more of the threshing. Ingenious men were already devising weird gadgets that resulted much later in a milking machine. Cream separators replaced the wide skimming pans. Plows were coming in gang-form, and you rode them. Horse-rakes appeared in self-dumping models. Improved balers compressed hay more quickly. The reaper added an automatic binder. It changed again to become a complete harvester that cut and threshed grain in one operation—the combine. A thousand failures brought machines that actually picked cotton, picked corn, picked sugar beets, dup potatoes, brought cultivators that worked deep or shallow; and planters and seeders that covered more land in a day than a man could cover in two weeks. Most of these wonderful machines have reached their peak of development only since the all-purpose tractor was perfected in the 1930's. Meanwhile, chemistry had performed almost magically in the realm of fertilizers and pest exterminators, though there is many a successful farmer who holds that fertilizer from the cow stable is superior to anything from the laboratory. Whoever is right, today's farmer produces far more than his father did, and with incomparably less hard labor. Progress seems so swift, and the "old days" so far off that many middle-aged farmers find a pleasant nostalgia in the scores of steam-power and horse-power threshing events that have become part of state and county fairs the country over.

HE INVENTED THE GAT, TOO. *Before devising the rapid-fire gun that bears his name, Richard J. Gatling of North Carolina invented several agricultural machines, including this horse-drawn drill for planting wheat.*

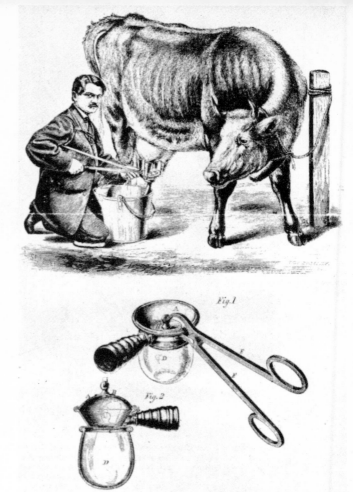

PARASOL FOR PLOW-BOYS. *Nothing in the record indicates that this patented umbrella ever became popular; but it does prove that inventors didn't overlook the poor husbandman.*

Almost a century ago, the august Scientific American displayed this milking machine—Calvin's Patent Breast Pump—as a wonderful example of the fruits of Yankee ingenuity. Old farmers agree that hand milking probably drove more men off the farm than any other task. This device was expected to stop that trend. It didn't.

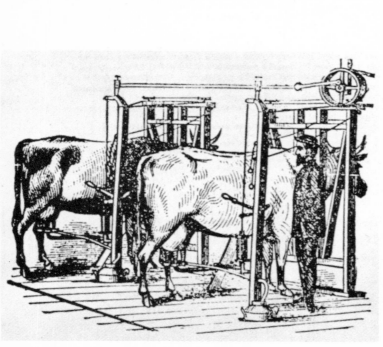

"IT IMITATES THE CALF . . ." *That's what the Hydraulic Cow-Milking Machine Co. said in 1868 of its patented rig which would "fit any cow" and was "simple, durable and self-adjusting." But the ideal mechanical milker did not appear until the 1920's.*

AIR POWER.
Windmills on farms were used chiefly for pumping water, but the U. S. Wind Engine & Pump Co. had a marvellous geared model for the top of the barn. It could be hooked up to run a corn sheller, feed mill, straw cutter, threshing machine and circular saw simultaneously, as made clear in this catalog of 1877.

COMBINED CULTIVATOR
COTTON & CORN PLANTER

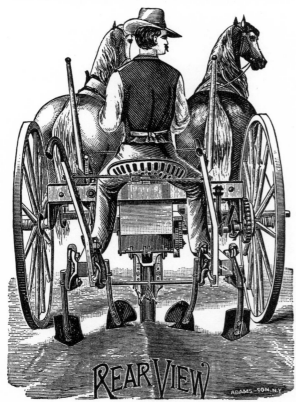

REAR VIEW

"STANDARD" ROTARY AND SLIDE HORSE CORN PLANTER.

Old-time farmers remember Emerson and Company, farm machine manufacturers, who became Emerson, Talcott and Company, then Emerson, Brantingham and was finally acquired by the J. I. Case Co. Their "standard" machines were among the best.

TRIAL OF MCCORMICK'S GRAIN CUTTING MACHINE. *In a field of oats on John Steele's farm in Rockbridge County, Virginia, Cyrus McCormick's newly patented reaper made history. Though an eyewitness of this event in 1831 said "nobody believed it would come to much," the machine was the genesis of the International Harvester Company of today.*

TEN-TON PLOW. *It looks like something out of Jules Verne, but it was a field locomotive actually manufactured in 1891 by Jacob Price, who hoped it would be the answer to the farmers' prayer for a steam-plowing rig.*

IT LIVED OFF THE COUNTRY. *The ideal steam engine for treeless and coalless prairies was one like this J. I. Case of 1886 which could be fuelled with waste straw. Made by all machinery houses, it was popular for three decades.*

EARLY COTTON PICKING MACHINE. *The mechanical harvesting of cotton presented many difficulties, and this machine, patented in 1885, was merely another step in the slow evolution which half a century later resulted in a successful picker powered by gasoline.*

PIONEER
AGRICULTURAL MACHINE SHOP,
South Salem, Oregon.

D. L. RIGGS, PROPRIETOR.

Particular Attention Given to Manufacturing and Repairing

THRESHERS, HEADERS, REAPERS, MOWERS, DRAPERS, or GRAIN BELTS,

Sickles, and all Kinds of Gear and Brass Castings, Belting, Canvas and Sheet Iron Work.

OLD MACHINES RENEWED AND IMPROVED. IMPROVED CYLINDER TEETH, THE BEST AND CHEAPEST.

Mill Work and Saw Smithing in all their Branches.   Patterns made, and Castings furnished to order.

| ALL KINDS OF
MODELS
MADE.
GEAR CUTTING
TO ORDER. | 
Molds to Mend Cracked or Broken Bells.
Patented June 16, 1874. | **BELLS MENDED**
—AND—
MADE AS GOOD AS NEW.
SHOP OR STATE RIGHTS
FOR SALE. |

With the machines, inevitably came the machine shops. Riggs apparently was busy, with four threshing machines and three headers awaiting repairs.

HARVESTING WITH STEAM POWER. *The black billow from the stack was impressive but too often the prairie was set afire by the sparks.*

IT DIDN'T WORK GOOD. *Soon or late, just about every farm machine was hooked to steam-power, but spraying with a steam engine proved both cumbersome and expensive, especially when horses had to pull the engine. This piece of equipment was soon replaced by a motorized sprayer.*

THRESHING TIME. *Before the days of the combine, a steam traction engine was belted to the threshing machine to operate the grain separator and also the wind-stacker. Shown here in full blow, the stacker is wafting straw and chaff into a pile while the clean grain is being sacked by the man second from right.*

Before vitamins were the fashion, the farmer cut his green cornstalks into ensilage and packed it by steam power in his silo to serve as winter feed.

The International Harvester Company's Titan was powered by oil, partly
to get away from the danger of prairie fires.

HOLT AND DEERE IN A DUET. *Beginning about 1910, gasoline tractors were entered in plowing contests to demonstrate that the day of steam was passing. This Holt crawler is pulling three pieces of John Deere disking equipment before an immense crowd at Walla Walla, Washington.*

MACHINE-AGE CASUALTY. *Overgrown with weeds, its whistle long silent, this steam threshing engine of 1869 was found eighty years later on a ranch on the Oregon-California border. It may well have reached the West Coast by way of the Horn.*

THE ROLLING HILLS OF OLD PALOUSE. *Because the Palouse country of Washington has long been celebrated for its wheat growing, farm machinery makers have always been ready to devise special equipment for the billowing terrain, like this combine built for side-hill work.*

Buggies & Shays . . . . Ferries & Sleighs

THE FARMER'S first roads were the trails that had been used by Indians and hunters, then by the postboys. Foot or horseback was the only way to travel them; but, widened a bit, the trails would admit passage of the two-wheeled shay (chaise) and the narrow sleds and sleighs and wagons of the period. Towns took the initiative in road improvement; and farmers "worked out" their taxes by labor, the use of their teams, or both. It was the little towns that built the first rude bridges, laid logs over swampy ground to make "corduroy," dug out boulders, felled trees, filled mud-holes with gravel, and often established a ferry. As the roads widened and improved, a variety of conveyances came into use. The farmer's first need was a plain, solid wagon for two horses, which was standard equipment until the gasoline truck. A common one-seated buggy with a top that could be raised and lowered was his everyday vehicle for a trip to town. For the worst roads, he might have a buckboard. In time, he could afford a two-seated surrey with a fringe around the top. This was his Sunday Best. (He left the victorias, the barouches, and other fancy rigs to the city people.)

The railroad changed his life in many ways. He did not have to drive so far to buy or sell, or to get his mail. Out on the treeless prairies, he might have to live in a house of sods before the railroad came; and burn buffalo and cow dung or straw until fuel could be shipped in. In an indirect way, too, the railroad, more than troops, "pacified" the Indians who harassed the settlers. With the rails laid, professional hunters quickly slaughtered the buffalo by the millions and shipped their hides to eastern markets, thereby removing the chief subsistence of the plains tribes. It was not, however, until after 1914 when, with the arrival of the cheap automobile, the farmer, like his city cousins, took to the road. Only then did roads become worthy of the name.

THE PRIZE—AN 1888 STUDEBAKER. *A crowd of farmers in Salt Lake City for a Prize Drawing on a wagon made by Studebaker, than which none had a finer reputation. Studebaker Brothers had their place right next door to the Zion Cooperative Mercantile Company, official store of the Latter-Day Saints.*

HUCKSTERISM IN THE 1880's. *The advertising boys of the E. D. Clapp Company lean heavily on the humor of exaggeration to sell Auburn farm wagons.*

THE AUBURN WAGON Is made at Auburn, N.Y. by THE E D CLAPP WAGON CO. LIMITED. AGENTS WANTED IN ALL UNOCCUPIED TERRITORY. Send for illustrated Circular and Price List.

"THE AUBURN" TAKES THE LEAD.
FARMER WATKINS WITH HIS PLOW TEAM AND AUBURN WAGON, GIVES THE BOY'S A BRUSH ON THE TROTTING PARK, AS USUAL "THE AUBURN" TAKES THE LEAD.

THE AUBURN WAGON IS SOLD AND WARRANTED BY

"STRONG AS AN OX." *Although driving a yoke of oxen with reins and bridles was not common, the Wisconsin turn-out below looks efficient if not elegant; and, anyway, elegance was served by the lady's flowered bonnet, not to speak of the fringed rug over her shoulders.*

RELAX, JESSIE. Nothing nicer on a fine day than a ride in the surrey behind old Jessie, the little Morgan. Mamma has got out to release the checkrein, thus giving the horse comfort in flytime.

FRINGE ON TOP. Sunbonnet Sue and her little sister pose in this classic surrey with the fringe on top, a vehicle usually reserved for better roading than that shown here. The surrey, whose name came from an English county, was a two-seater but might not have a top at all.

ONE-HORSE SHAY.
*A country doctor in his
open-seater buggy.*

WHIPS AND WHIP SOCKET. *No rig was complete without them, and they
were taken so much for granted that on the earliest automobiles whip
sockets were standard equipment.*

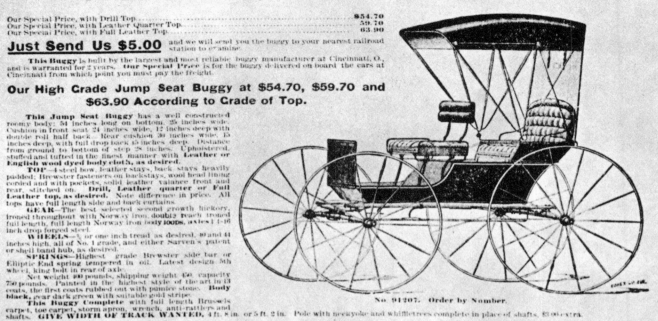

OUR SPECIAL $54.70 JUMP SEAT BUGGY.

Our Special Price, with Drill Top $54.70
Our Special Price, with Leather Quarter Top 59.70
Our Special Price, with Full Leather Top 63.90

Just Send Us $5.00 and we will send you the buggy to your nearest railroad station to examine.

This Buggy is built by the largest and most reliable buggy manufacturer at Cincinnati, O., and is warranted for 2 years. Our Special Price is for the buggy delivered on board the cars at Cincinnati from which point you must pay the freight.

Our High Grade Jump Seat Buggy at $54.70, $59.70 and $63.90 According to Grade of Top.

This Jump Seat Buggy has a well constructed roomy body; 54 inches long on bottom, 25 inches wide. Cushion in front seat 24 inches wide, 12 inches deep with double roll half back. Rear cushion 30 inches wide, 15 inches deep, with full drop back 15 inches deep. Distance from ground to bottom of step 28 inches. Upholstered, stuffed and tufted in the finest manner with Leather or English wool dyed body cloth, as desired.

TOP—4 steel bow, leather stays, back stays heavily padded; Brewster fasteners on backstays, wool head lining corded and with pockets, solid leather valance front and rear, stitched on. Drill, Leather quarter or Full Leather top, as desired. Note difference in price. All tops have full length side and back curtains.

GEAR—The best selected second growth hickory, ironed throughout with Norway iron, double reach ironed full length, full length Norway iron body loops, axles 1 1-16 inch drop forged steel.

WHEELS—⅞ or one inch tread as desired, 40 and 44 inches high, all of No. 1 grade, and either Sarven's patent or shell band hub, as desired.

SPRINGS—Highest grade Brewster side bar or Elliptic End spring tempered in oil. Latest design 5th wheel, king bolt in rear of axle.

Net weight 90 pounds, shipping weight 450, capacity 750 pounds. Painted in the highest style of the art in 13 coats, the first coats rubbed out with pumice stone. Body black, gear dark green with suitable gold stripe.

This Buggy Complete with full length Brussels carpet, toe carpet, storm apron, wrench, anti-rattlers and shafts. GIVE WIDTH OF TRACK WANTED, 4 ft. 8 in. or 5 ft. 2 in. Pole with neckyoke and whiffletrees complete in place of shafts, $3.00 extra.

Understand the above picture shows this jump seat buggy with front seat extended and as such can be used as a two seat rig for 4 people. When closed it is at once converted into a one-seated buggy. Our Offer to Ship C. O. D., Subject to Examination, ought to induce you to place your order, and if you send for this buggy we are sure we will sell more in your neighborhood.

No. 91207. Order by Number.

COMPLETE WITH BRUSSELS CARPET. $54.70 was a lot of money and you had to consider every detail before you ordered one delivered "on board the cars."

RATES OF TOLL.

For Every Wagon, Cart or Carriage or Buggy Drawn by 1 Horse		5¢
" " " " " Drawn by 2 Horses or Oxen		10 "
" " Horse in Addition		3 "
" " Sled or Sleigh Drawn by 1 Horse		4 "
" " " " " 2 Horses		6 "
" " Horse in Addition		3 "
" " Horse and Rider		4 "
" " Horse, Mule or Ass Led or Driven		1 "
" " Head of Neat Cattle		⅓ "
" " " " Sheep or Hogs		⅙ "
" " Stage Coach, Hack or Omnibus Drawn by 2 Horses		12 "
" " Horse in Addition		3 "
" " Bicycle, Tricycle or Velocipede		4 "

TOLL ROADS AND TOLL BRIDGES. These rates, posted in Ohio around the turn of the century, were about average.

GLAMOR-RIG. *Outside the circus, one seldom saw four horses abreast, such as pulled this 3½-seater buckboard, a limber vehicle that bounced and bucked and feared neither ruts nor stones.*

ELEGANT HAYRIDE. *It wasn't all buggy, or even all horse, and this hayride party moved in a rick behind oxen with brass tips and bows on their horns, while the teamster, goadstick in hand, wore a plug hat.*

In winter the milk went to town or railroad depot behind the Bay and the Dapple on a bobsled with ironshod runners that wailed when frosty and froze if left standing long.

Fixed up with boards, the bobsled would accommodate a score of ladies for a gay ride on the new snow.

NO FRINGE. *The covered buggy built for all roads and seasons had no fancy fringe on top. It was a rugged rig that could take hub-high mud and go anywhere a stout team could pull it.*

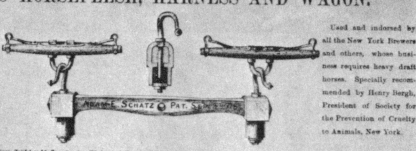
THE OLD GRAY MARE, SHE . . . *If you were using a heavy wagon in 1878, you would do well to get one of these patent whiffletrees, highly endorsed by the SPCA.*

NOT DEAD—JUST MIRED. *Even two horses could not pull the buggy through this Missouri mud of half a century ago. The other animal has obviously cleared itself, and will doubtless be hitched to its mate's collar to pull it from the mire.*

"It Arched the Flood . . ." Wet or dry, most roads sooner or later passed through a covered bridge, such as this sturdy one still in use at Tunbridge Market, Vermont.

Low Bridge, and Long. Sheltered in winter and shaded in summer, a covered bridge was always a welcome experience, even though you had to walk your horse or pay two dollars. This one, a wood truss structure, was of unusual length.

Working-Bridge. The farmer often had to bridge a stream to get to his own fields. He built for strength, not beauty.

THE FAMOUS DITCH. The Erie Canal was a highway to the edge of the West, and over it returned the produce of the frontier farmers.

WHEAT GOING DOWN-RIVER. The Sternwheeler Varuna and a loaded wheat barge of the Sacramento River fleet in California, ready to head downstream where the grain could be stored at Martinez, or Port Chicago, or transferred directly to some deep-sea vessel for shipment abroad.

FERRY BY HAND. *This home-made ferry across Florida's Ocklawaha River was operated by hand. Although it might ride the river well, a wise traveller would steady his horse or team while the craft was in motion.*

PRIMITIVE FERRY. *Up to recently several thousand ferry craft operated on American rivers, like this one at High Bridge, Kentucky, which appears to be carrying a Rural Free Delivery rig.*

WAITING FOR THE CARS. *Standing stark in the midst of Nebraska space, this typical depot was contact with the world beyond the quarter-sections of range grass or wheat. There you could send out a message by Western Union, and there Wells, Fargo could bring you almost anything. And the never-failing wind ran the trackside pump that watered the Iron Horse.*

THE FAST MAIL. *To the endless awe of the spectators, a fast train of the Lake Shore & Michigan Southern does not even slow down to drop one mail bag and pick up another.*

THE CARRIAGE WITHOUT HORSES. *As long ago as 1914, photographers were alert to the contrast between the new and the old, to the handwriting on the wall that said that the horse was about to disappear.*

Schooldays, Schooldays...

MORE OFTEN than not, farm children attended a one-room district school that was painted red. (Red paint lasted longer than white.) Usually they walked to school, carrying with them their lunches in bright handsome five-pound pails that once held lard. There were no school lunches. Even teacher brought hers and ate it cold, with water fetched by favored pupils from a nearby spring. It was customary for the schoolmarm to "board around," first with one family, then another. She taught all the grades from first to eighth, or whatever the final grade before high school was numbered. Pupils sat two-by-two at wooden desks, often well carved with the initials of their own fathers and mothers. The heating system was a box stove, fairly toasting the first rows, leaving the back rows to shiver. Reading, writing and 'rithmetic were the main studies, though history and geography were included. Every child had a slate; there was no paper to waste. The blackboard was important; it was not only a medium for visual study but also for discipline. You might be kept after school to write on it, over and over again, the undeniable fact that "Our First President was George Washington." On the last day of the school year it was proper that Teacher treat everyone to candy, and for the pupils to speak pieces like "Curfew Shall Not Ring Tonight," "Horatius at the Bridge," or "Paul Revere's Ride." Though the teaching may have been poor, the lighting bad, and the crowding worst of all, the Little Old Red Schoolhouse went into American legend as the classic font of learning in the United States.

Time for Reading and 'Riting and 'Rithmetic.

SOD-HOUSE SCHOOL. *Typical of Wyoming as well as Nebraska schools in the Eighties was this one built of the only construction material available before the railroad came. Slabs were cut from the prairie, piled one upon the other, and roofed with a few planks or poles and another layer of sod.*

LOG CABIN SCHOOL. *An early Florida school still using rough-hewn log construction.*

SCHOOL BEGINS. *The first day of school was, in many places, clean-up day. The kids came with rakes and shovels to gather up the dead leaves, sticks and stones and trash that had accumulated during the summer.*

SNOWBALL TIME. *The pupils of District School Number 24 of Proctor, Montana, take time out from fun in the snow to have their pictures taken.*

SEAT OF LEARNING. *Children's ages in a one-room school, such as this one in Vermo[n]t more than fifty years ago, ranged from five [to] twenty. Desks were for three pupils eac[h] these, obviously, had been decorated by ge[n]erations of jack-knife art.*

STAGE TO SCHOOL. *The school bus, of exactly two-horse power, was called a stage and into it climbed the kids of a dozen farms along the route. The lucky boy beside the driver operated the brake.*

...and Playtime

YOUNG FRY on the farm lived in a marvellous world of bright fields, dark woods, talking brooks, and ponds like mirrors. Its center was The Barn, a gigantic playhouse of rafters, haymows, stables, pens, granaries; of sliding doors, trap-doors, doors big enough to ride on, doors that opened for monstrous wagons; of swallows darting through the bird holes in the gables, bringing food to their young in the mud nests under the roof; of squeaking barn mice, and the half-wild barn cats who never went near the farmhouse; and now and then a sinister weasel bent on slaughtering hens. The Barn was also permeated with a pleasant though indescribable aroma which was never to be forgotten. Perhaps the greatest privilege of farm youngsters was the right to go barefoot half the year, to sqush mud up through toes, to toughen feet until they could walk over stiff new stubble and never feel it. The swimming hole was always near, and the diving board was a boulder that once was used as a slide by playful otters. The brook held speckled trout; the creek might have perch, surely catfish (or bullheads). Even a Wyoming buffalo wallow would float a raft. The woods was alive with game for bow-and-arrow, for the Daisy air rifle, and the adult 22-Winchester. There were caves, doubtless of pirates or smugglers, to be explored. Any old elm had crotches to climb and to hold a tree-house. Almost any young farm animal was a potential pet. Of formal games there was London Bridge, Ring-Around-a-Rosey, I-Spy, and of course Pump-Pump-Pull Away. There were also chores to do, and it is probable that farm youngsters had more responsibilities than average city children. But whether or not they knew it—and doubtless they did—farm children lived right in the center of a superlative playground.

"SNAP THE WHIP." The little Red Schoolhouse and boys at play in this painting by Boston-born Winslow Homer created something of a sensation when exhibited at the Philadelphia Exposition of 1876. Though generally famous as America's finest marine artist, Homer was also known for nostalgic pictures of country life.

PLAY BALL! The Great American Game recruited many famous professionals from cow-pasture leaguers like these farm boys playing baseball where a hazard of left field is a manure spreader and several wagons. Cy Young (Ohio) and Ty Cobb (Georgia) learned to play on just such rural diamonds.

HOME-MADE THREE-WHEELER. Most farm boys could make almost anything from this and that picked up here and there. It might be a fishing-hook from a bent pin or a bicycle made of old wagon wheels and a discarded bike-front.

BARNYARD GAME. The rules of barn-ball were elastic, but the idea was for one player to bounce a ball against a barn wall and for the other to hit it with a bat on the rebound. The batter here is wearing laced canvas leggings that probably belonged to an older brother in the Army of 1917-18.

All a youngster needed to perform marvels on a trout stream were an alder
pole, some string, that bent pin and a can of worms.

A group of youngsters, waiting for the buckboard that will take them to the picnic grounds, pose dutifully for the picture-man.

It was good to sit on the bridge, kicking your toes in the cool water, or watching the minnows swimming round and round the little cleared space where the fish eggs were.

Huck Finn on his raft was just any American country boy.

There were other places to swim, besides the "ol' swimmin' hole" but you'd
have to wear a bathing suit if you went swimming
in a wide-open place like this.

"Howdy, Stranger."

"I'll be your bashful, barefoot beau."

They were even better
when they were
stolen, even though
you didn't wait for the
cherries or apples or
peaches to be
quite ripe.

TEETER-TOTTER.
A plank, a log, and two pair of springy young legs.

No matter that crickets crawled down your neck and grasshoppers got into your hair, riding a load of new mown hay was fun and filled with the aroma of the farm in midsummer.

Saluting the Fourth *with a fusillade of cap-pistols and blank cartridges in an open field . . .*

. . . or with a giant firecracker in the village street.

SLEEPING IT OFF. *Carving out the Jack-o'-Lantern for Hallowe'en was hard work.*

Buying and Selling

THE FARMER was periodically offered merchandise at his very door. On foot came pack-peddlers, trudging the roads that were snow, or mud, or dust, carrying a load fit for a horse, sleeping in barns, eating where they could, and bringing to the farms an assortment of cheap jewelry, bright scarves and handkerchiefs, needles, thread, and other "notions." But for most everyday needs the farmer went to "the store."

Here and there the old-fashioned Country Store survives and even flourishes in spite of mail-order houses and highways. Once upon a time this general emporium, as it was sometimes called, was the farmer's sole contact with business. During its long heyday it was the place where he sold his produce and got in return the merchandise or store-goods he needed. It stood in every village and at many a crossroads. The typical country store was a great rambling building, the lower floor with conventional shelves and counters, the upper a home for the merchant, or perhaps a hall for dances, entertainments and meetings. Usually attached to the main structure was a long ell with big doors and an outside platform where barrels of flour and molasses and crackers could be loaded to farm wagons or sleds. Cattle feed, too, was loaded here. The enchantment of the country store was in its fragrance and its eye-arresting variety of display. Here in one great gorgeous room were the blended scents of the Orient, of South America, of Virginia and Kentucky, plus a whiff of Standard Oil; and the sights encompassed virtually every need of man, woman and child. Buggy whips hung above a showcase of ribbons. Cant-dogs stood in a corner with linoleum, near the yardage goods. Straw hats were suspended above rows of patent medicines whose labels testified to cures almost beyond belief. The huge coffee mill stood as brilliant as a fire engine. Salt cod was piled like cordwood. Corsets crowded chewing-tobacco. Boots and shoes crawled among the kitchen ware. In the middle of everything was the village postoffice, its front a wall of little boxes with windowpanes, its sides of chicken-wire. Before it stood a big barrel stove, a couple of chairs, a box of sawdust. Here was the Village Forum. And here in one barnlike room was concentrated the life of the town as it touched matters social, medical, civic, and mercantile. Nothing can quite replace it.

THE YANKEE PEDDLER. *The so-called Yankee Peddlers usually came in a special wagon. It jingled and glinted with tinware, and its sides were amazing scenes painted in cardinal colors. Inside was an astonishing array of merchandise, including clocks, muslins, taffetas, bombazines; medicines good for man or beast, patent apple-parers, calf-weaners, rings for bulls and boars, books by Mrs. Stowe, Lew Wallace, Mrs. E. D. E. N. Southworth, together with a thick Home Medical Adviser, and Bibles big and medium, each with a handsome Family Record to note births, weddings, and "removals." Almost as familiar as the peddler was the Lightning-Rod Man, who often posed as a good samaritan who merely wanted you to protect your home from the wrath of God in the form of electric storms. There were also out-and-out fakers trying to sell "states rights" for worthless patents on churns and such; and agents peddling the seeds of "Bohemian Hulless Oats" which would make your fortune.*

"It stood in every village, and at many a crossroads."

COUNTRY STORE. *The center of things in hamlet and village was likely to be the general store, shown here as it looked in 1873 to the Vermont genre painter, Thomas Waterman Wood. Barter was still a medium of exchange (note the eggs). The storekeeper was the U. S. Postmaster. And around the store stove sectional and national issues were debated by the local experts.*

Great Inducements!

TO GRANGES, FARMERS' CLUBS, OR ANY OTHER MAN!

Upon application, we will mail FREE, to ANYBODY who orders or buys
any of the articles named below, a copy of

"OUR CHROMO,"

THE CHEAP-HORSE CORN PLANTER!

The above represented machine has been patented and perfected, after much trouble and expense, by the inventor, who fondly hopes it will meet the growing demand for a **CHEAP-HORSE PLANTER**, which is fully warranted, thusly: If the Cheap-Horse part does not work satisfactorily, the planters can be detached from the horse's legs, and you have a couple of **R. F. Batcheller's Celebrated Hand Corn Planters**, which everybody knows will work well in all cases, and can be furnished by us in any amount. Send in your orders early.

Below we give a partial list of our principal articles, which we invite the public generally to examine before purchasing elsewhere:

The Avery Stalk Cutter,
The Star Corn Planter,
The Vandiver Corn Planter,
Furst & Bradley's Walking and Riding Cultivators,
Furst & Bradley's Harrows and Scrapers,
Furst & Bradley's Stirring & Breaking Plows,
Furst & Bradley's Sulky Hay Rakes,
B. D. Buford & Co.'s Stirring and Breaking Plows,
B. D. Buford & Co.'s Gang Plows,
B. D. Buford & Co.'s Black Hawk Cultivators,
Champion Cultivators,
La Harpe Cultivators,
Gorham Riding Cultivator,
Gorham Seeders,
Lowth & Howe's Broadcast Seeders,
Cahoon Hand and Power Seeders,
"New Departure" Tongueless Cultivators,
Bain, Newton, and Rock Falls Wagons,
Cincinnati 3-spring Wagons,
Michigan and Chicago Farm Pumps,
Battle Creek Vibrators,
Champion Reapers and Mowers,
Eward Harvesters,
Low, Adams and French Harvester,
Haines, Illinois Headers,
Bear's Gang Plows,
Brown's Corn Planters, (for Madison,
Guthrie, and Adair counties,)
Step and Extension Ladders,
Broom Handles,
Wire and Twine,
Cane Mills,
Blossburg and Lehigh Coal,

Doty's Washing Machine,
Peerless Clothes Wringer,
Comstock's Garden Drill,
(with all attachments),
Blanchard's Churns,
Feed Cutters,
Farmers' Boilers,
Farm and Warehouse Fan Mills (all sizes),
Perkins' Wind Mills,
Feed Grinders,
Hand and Power Corn Shellers,
Ox Yokes,
Cider Mills,
Cider Presses,
Stoves and Tinware,
Hardware and Nails,
A full line of Wagon and Buggy Stock,
both Green and Dry,
Clover Seed,
Timothy Seed,
Osage Orange Seed,
Onion Seed,
Onion Sets,
Kentucky Blue Grass,
Red Top,
Millet,
Hungarian,
Seed Wheat, and a
Full Line of Garden and Flower Seeds,
Lawn Mowers,
Galvanized Iron and Copper
Lightning Rods, and material,
at Wholesale or Retail.

Western Farm Journal
SUPPLEMENT.
FRIDAY, APRIL 3, 1874.

A Western Granger has written for some Mardi Gras seed "Why was the whale that swallowed Jonah like a jolly milkman?" Because he got a profit (prophet) out of the water.

Among the attractions of a sale of oil paintings advertised in San Francisco is a picture of Gen. Jackson just from the bath.

A Kentucky farmer refused to look at a sample sewing machine not long ago, as he always "sewed" by hand. He is related to the man who did not want a threshing machine on his farm, "for," said he, "give me a harness fog or a barrel stave and I can make my family toe the mark according to the law and scripter."

QUANTITY OF SEEDS REQUIRED PER ACRE.

Wheat	1½ to 2	bushels
Rye	1½	
Oats	2½	
Barley	2½	
Peas	2 to 3	
White beans	1½	
Buckwheat	¾	
Corn, broadcast	4	
Corn, in drills	4 to 12	quarts
Corn, in hills	4 to 8	
Broom corn	1	bushel
Potatoes	10 to 15	bushel
Beets	5	pounds
Carrots	3	
Ruta bagas	2	
Millet	½	bushel
Clover, white	4	quarts
Clover, red	8	
Timothy	6	
Orchard grass	2	bushels
Red-top	1 to 2	pecks
Blue grass	2	bushels
Mixed lawn grass	1 to 2	
Tobacco		ounces

FARMERS' AND MECHANICS' SUPPLIES OF ALL KINDS.

Circulars or Information concerning the above articles furnished upon application. Orders by Mail Solicited, and Promptly Attended to, and Lowest Prices Guaranteed.

Cor. Cour. Av. and 2d St.,
DES MOINES, IOWA.

E. E. AINSWORTH.   J. S. BONBRIGHT.

POST ME UP.

THE AD-MAN'S HUMOR WAS BROAD. *Even the dullest witted could see from this ad that he could not get along without Vacuum Harness Oil.*

GOOD FOR MAN OR BEAST. *Advertisements might be of a comic-strip nature, but they made clear that the right medicine, such as Barker's Nerve & Bone Linament, would perform wonders and acted alike on man and beast.*

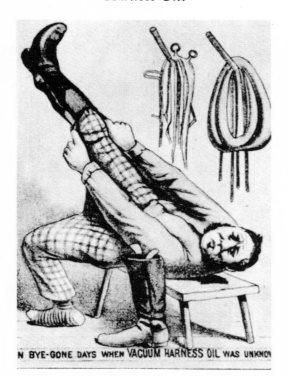

IT CURED ALL ILLS. *Only one of thousands of patent medicines with which Americans dosed themselves. Here a Good Samaritan in buckskin is dispensing from a sack bulging with bottles of Dr. Girard's elixir.*

THE ASSURANCE OF AGE. *Only a long-established firm could afford so modest a claim.*

THE FRUITS OF HUSBANDRY IN WYOMING. The prize committee has already attached award tickets to these, the grandest pumpkins, cabbages and potatoes in Big Horn County.

HOME-GROWN, BIGGEST AND BEST. A main attraction at all county fairs was the Agricultural Hall. Second to none in Nebraska were these entries from Box Butte County.

MARKET DAY. Back in the 1850's German immigrants in Watertown, Wisconsin, began to hold a cattle fair and market day on the second Tuesday of each month. Native Americans liked the idea, too, and the event was something of a commercial and festive occasion for more than half a century.

One effect of the phenomenal spread of railroads in the latter part of the last century was the rise of the business of selling goods by mail. A. Montgomery Ward of Chicago founded the first of the big houses and dedicated his earliest catalog to members of the Patrons of Husbandry, or Grange. From that time to this farmers have been the most important customers of Ward, Sears, Roebuck and other mail-order houses, a development made possible not only by the railroads but also by parcel post and RFD.

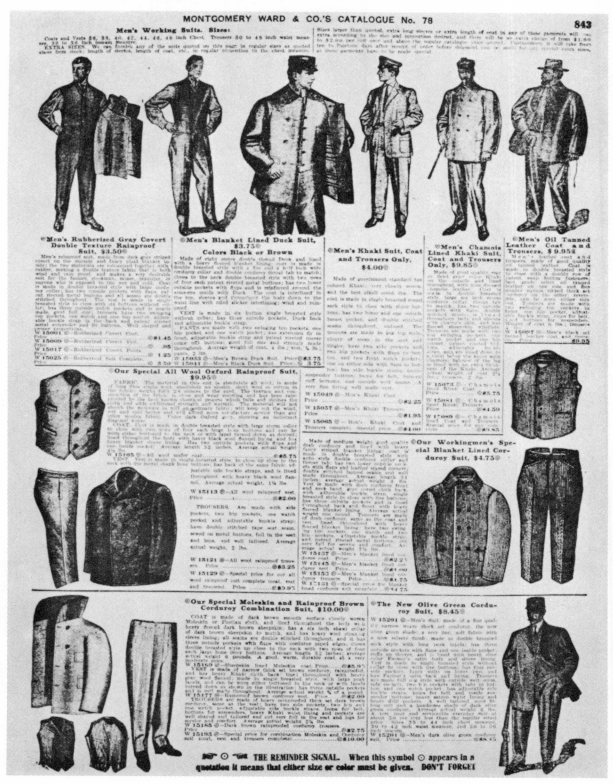

Roasting Pans Continued.

(See previous page.)

No. 16447. Self-basting Roasting Pan, with sliding cover and open end, the only first-class roaster and baker on the market, having a grate to keep the roast from the bottom of the pan, and a door at the end for browning to any desired extent a person may wish, and can be looked into without removing from the oven, as the cover slides on the pan. Made from the best iron, will last, if properly cared for, ten years or more.

No.,	2	3	4	5
Length,	13	15	16	18½
Width,	9	10	11	13
Height,	7	8	9	10
Price, each,	$0.60	.80	.85	1.10

PIECED WATER DIPPERS.

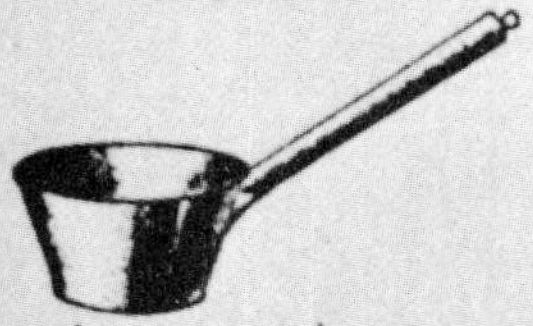

No. 16454. Pieced tin Water Dippers, with copper bottom. Size, 2 quarts. Price, each, 10c; per dozen, $1.10.

GALVANIZED IRON DIPPERS.

Manufacturers' measure will not hold as much as represented.

No. 16455. Price, each, 1 quart, 7c; 2 quarts, 10c; 3 quarts, 11c.

BISCUIT AND CAKE CUTTERS.

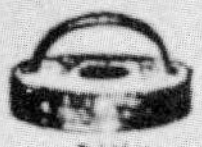

16459

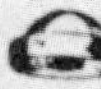

16460

No. 16459. Biscuit Cutters. Size, 3x1 inches. Each, 3c; per doz., 25c.

No. 16460. Doughnut Cutters. Size, 3x1 inches. Each, 4c; per doz., 40c.

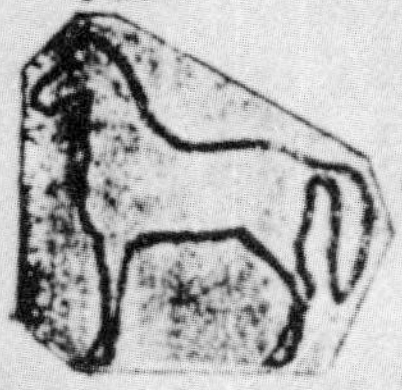

No. 16462. Cake Cutters, animals and birds, assorted styles. Each, 4c; per doz., 36c.

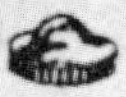

No. 16463. Cake Cutters, fancy assorted styles. Each, 4c; per doz., 40c.

PASTE JAGGERS.

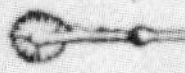

No. 16464. Tinned Paste Jaggers. Each, 5c; per doz., 54c.

APPLE CORERS.

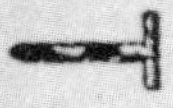

No. 16465. Price, each, 4c; per doz., 40c.

BOX GRATERS.

No. 16466. Patented Nutmeg Grater, japanned. Each, 3c; per doz., 30c.

RADISH GRATERS.

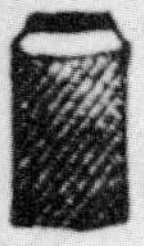

16467

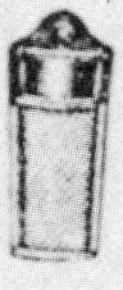

16466

No. 16467.

Size,	3x6½	4x9½	6x12
Each,	$0.04	.05	.08
Per doz.,	.42	.55	.85

TIN HORNS.

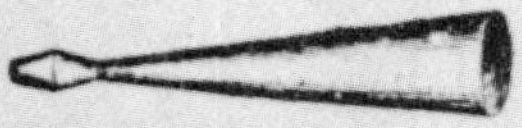

No. 16472. Tin Dinner Horns. Length, 13 inches, each, 6c; 22 inches, 15c.

FLOUR SIEVE.

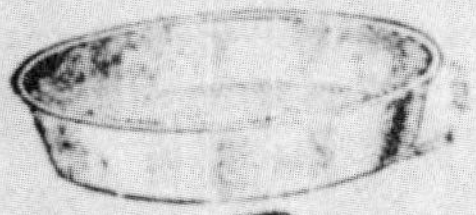

No. 16476. Tin rim Sieve, 12½ inches diameter, well put together, made of heavy tin. Each, 12c.

FLOUR SIFTER.

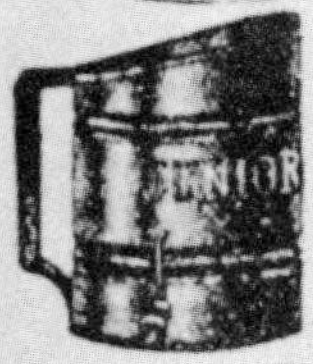

No. 16477. Rotary Flour Sifter, also serves as a scoop. Full size, well made, each, 10c.

EGG BEATERS.

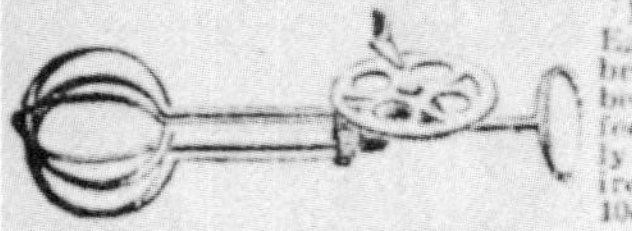

No. 16480. Dover Egg Beater. Celebrated as the best beater made; perfect action, strongly made, duplex iron frame. Each, 10c; per doz., $1.08.

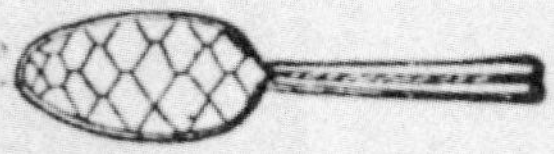

No. 16481. Surprise Egg Beater, retinned. Each, 3c.

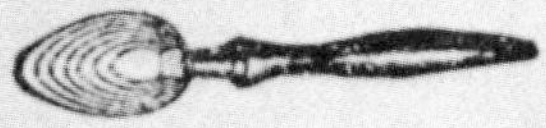

No. 16482. Spoon Egg Whip, with wood handle. Each, 4c.

SCOOPS.

No. 16483. Tin Scoops, retinned. Weight from ½ to 2 lbs.

Size,	6¾x4¼	8x5½	10x6½	11¾x7
Price, each,	$0.10	.12	.15	.20
Per doz.,	.90	1.20	1.45	1.80

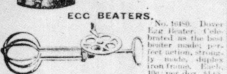

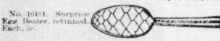

JAPANNED WARE.

CHAMBER PAILS.

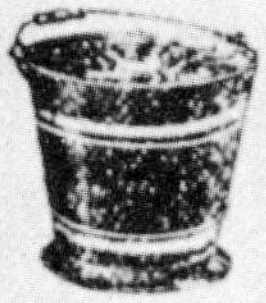

No. 16494. Slop Pail. Full size, elegantly painted outside and in, with double gilt band, tight fitting top or tray. Each, 30c.

No. 16495. Galvanized iron Chamber Pail. Made of heavy iron, will not rust. Each, 40c.

CHAMBER SETS.

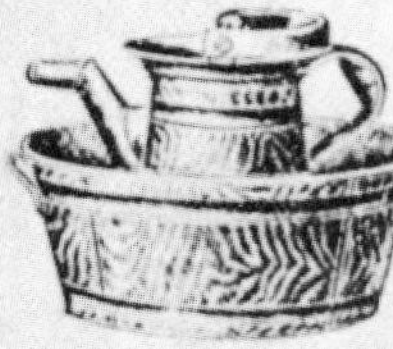

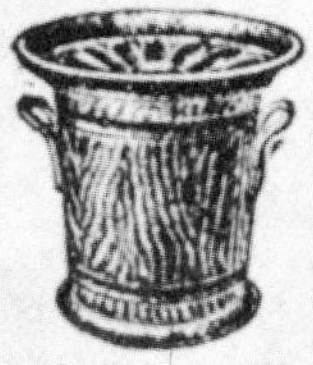

No. 16496. Chamber Sets. Full size, nicely finished in different styles, as follows: Oak, walnut, red and blue. Price, per set of 3 pieces, $1.30.

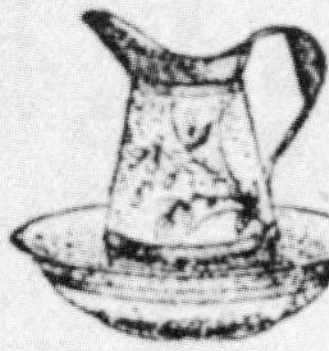

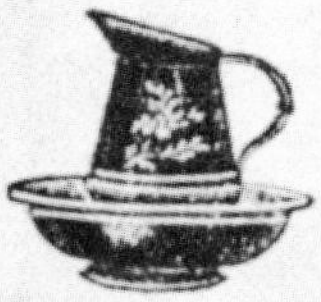

BOWL AND PITCHER.

No. 16497. Decorated Bowl and Pitcher. Beautiful and artistic designs, elegant workmanship, high, rich colors. Price, per set, 84c.

No. 16498. Bowl and Pitcher. Very heavy tin, painted in assorted colors; pretty set. Price, per set, 50c.

TOILET STAND.

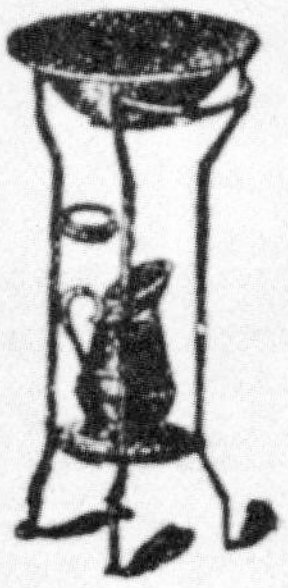

No. 16499. Toilet Stand, japanned. 30½ inches high, with japanned tin wash bowl and pitcher and soap cup, assorted colors; weight, 22½ lbs. Each, complete, $1.50.

BATH TUBS.

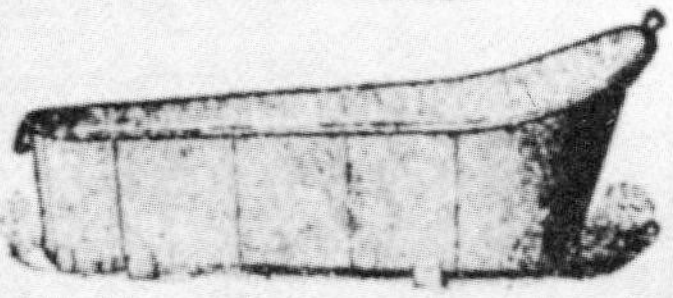

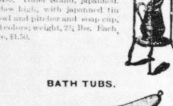

No. 16501. Plunge Baths; same shape as cut, made of heavy tin, with wooden bottoms and handles at each end; japanned, blue inside, drab outside, trimmed with black, blue and gilt stripes; weight, 50 lbs. Prices include crating. Each, 4 feet, $4.00; 6 feet, $5.50.

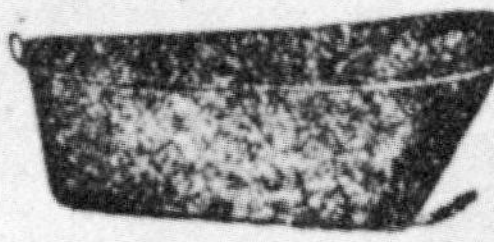

No. 16505. Infants' Bath Tub; weight, 10 to 25 lbs.; japanned tin. Size, 27 inch, 96c; 30 inch, $1.05; 33 inch, $1.25; 36 inch, $1.45.

HIP BATHS.

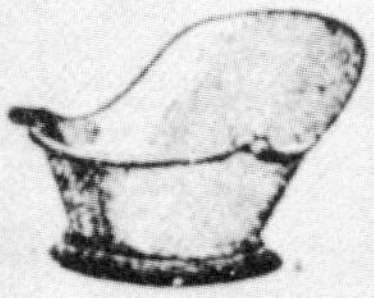

No. 16506. Japanned Hip Baths. Diameter, 22½ inches, each, $3.50; diameter, 27 inches, each, $4.25.

JAPANNED FOOT TUBS.

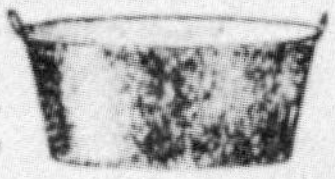

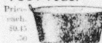

No. 16508.

Size.	Weight.	Price each.
17x13½x7½	2 lbs.	$0.45
18½x14½x8¼	2 lbs.	.50

SPITTOONS.

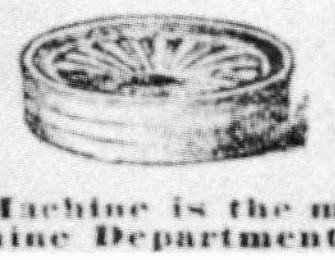

No. 16512. Spittoons, japanned, assorted colors. Each, 16c.

No. 16514. Gilt Decorated Cuspidor. Handsome gilt decoration. Price, each, 20c.

PROTECTION CUSPIDORS.

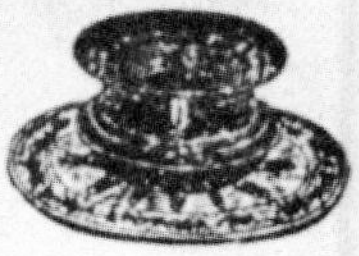

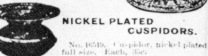

No. 16518. Handsomely ornamented and secured to a mat 12 inches in diameter; cannot be tipped over; can be detached from the mat for cleaning. Three colors, blue, green and red; japanned. No. 1, each, 24c.

NICKEL PLATED CUSPIDORS.

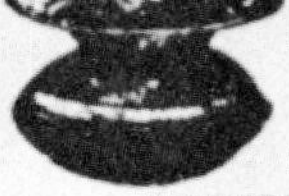

No. 16519. Cuspidor, nickel plated full size. Each, 35c.

CRUMB PANS AND BRUSH.

No. 16524. Crumb Tray and Brush. Handsomely decorated; brush made of pure bristles. Price, per set, 20c.

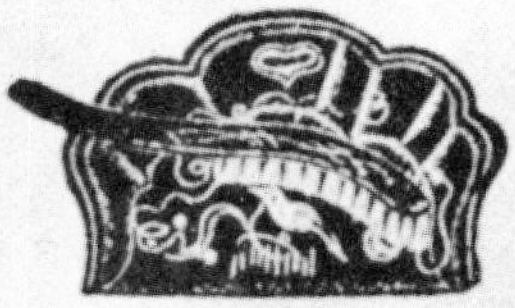

No. 16525. Brass Crumb Tray and Brush. Each, 62c.

No. 16526. Polished brass, nickel plated. Each, 80c.

TEA TRAY.

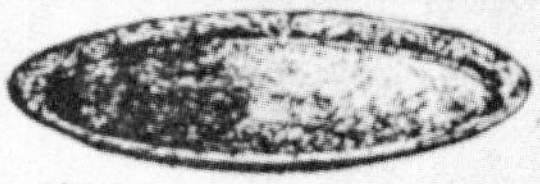

No. 16530. Tea Trays, oval, japanned.

Inches,	12	14	16	18	20
Each,	$0.12	.15	.18	.23	.25
Inches,	22	24	26	28	
Each,	.30	.37	.47	.57	

CHILD'S TRAY.

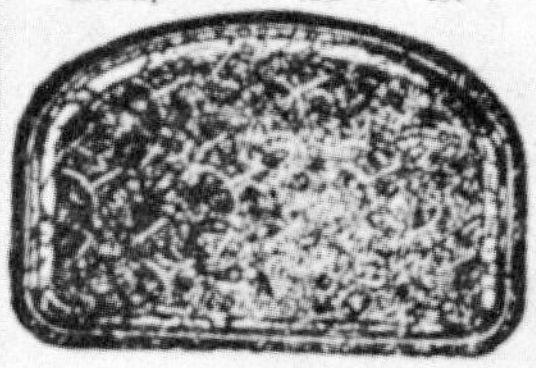

No. 16531. The Crown Child's Tray, silver finish, the best and cheapest child's tray made; complete with springs. Ready to adjust to table or high chair. Price, each, 18c.

PITCHER TRAY.

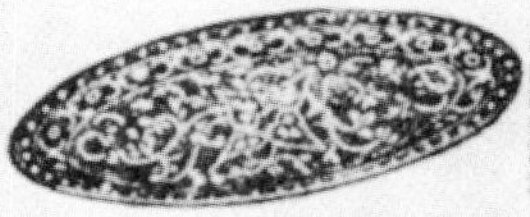

No. 16534. Round solid brass Tray, 13-inch fancy hammered brass tray, pretty pattern, beaded edges, highly polished. Each 25c.

DUST PANS.

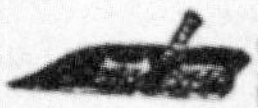

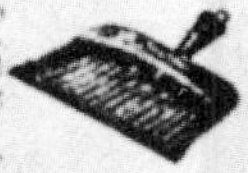

No. 16538. Whole sheet Dust Pan, Japanned; handle well braced, good, strong pan. Each, 8c.

No. 16540. Dust Pan, plain brown, covered. Each, 12c.

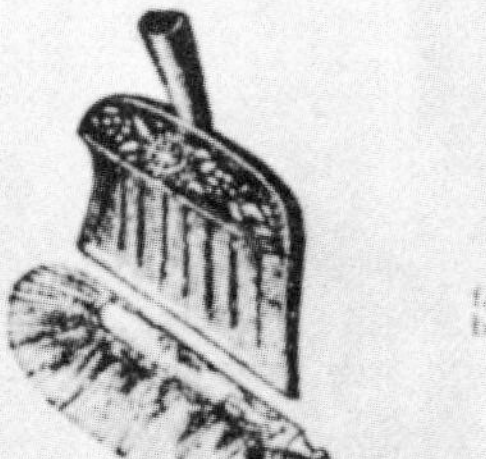

No. 16541. Dust Pan, fancy assorted colors, with brush. Each, 33c.

CANISTERS.

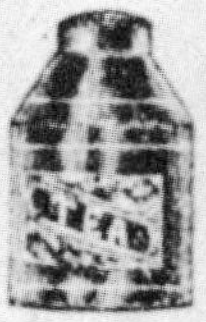

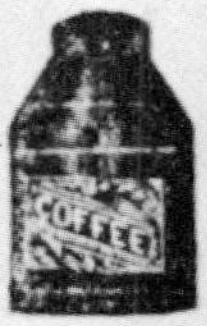

Japanned Tea or Coffee Canister.

No. 16550. Tea Canister.

No. 16551. Coffee Canister.

To hold 1 lb., each, 7c; doz., 76c.

To hold 2 lbs., each, 9c; doz., $1.05.

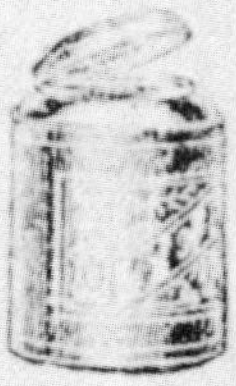

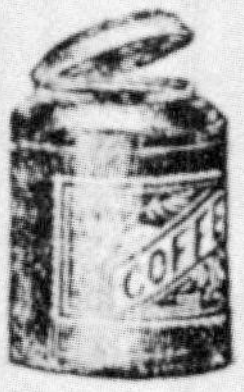

Tea and Coffee Canisters, japanned tin, with hinged covers. These canisters are preferable to the ordinary kind, as the covers cannot get lost.

No. 16552. Tea Canister.

No. 16553. Coffee Canisters.

To hold 2 lbs., each, 10c; doz., $1.08.

To hold 4 lbs., each, 15c; doz., $1.55.

Our special Drop Desk Cabinet Sewing Machine is the most desirable piece of household furniture ever sold. Look at it in the Sewing Machine Department, note the price and you will agree with us.

Feather Bang

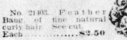

No. 21403. Feather Bang, of fine natural curly hair. See cut.
Each $2.50

No. 21403

No. 21404

No. 21404. Princess Bang, made of natural curly hair on weft; a popular bang, being light and easily attached. Each $0.50

Emma Wave.

No. 21406

No. 21406. Emma Wave, invisible hair lace foundation, natural curly hair, 3 inch part, 12 inches from side to side. Each, until sold $3.00

No. 21407. Kid Hair Curlers, neat and nice for curling the hair; 12 in package.

No. 21407.

Length	3½ in.	4 in.	4½ in.
Per package.	$0.06	$0.08	$0.10

Extraordinary values in Human Hair Switches.

No. 21408. Short Stem Hair Switches, in all ordinary and medium shades; extra shades will cost from 25 to 50 per cent. extra.

Weight About.	Length About.	Price, each
2 ounces	20 inches	$0.65
2 ounces	20 inches	0.90
2 ounces	22 inches	1.25
2 ounces	24 inches	1.50
3 ounces	24 inches	2.25
3½ ounces	26 inches	3.25

NOTE.—The above 65c. switch has long stem.

French hair switches can be made to order from $5.00 to $10.00 each.

No. 21409. Gray Hair Switches, fine quality, short stem. Be sure to send sample of hair.

Weight	Length	Each.
2 ounces	18 inches	$1.75
2½ ounces	22 inches	3.00
3 ounces	24 inches	4.00
3 ounces	25 inches	6.00

NOTE.—The above prices are for medium shades of gray. Where extra white is ordered it will cost ¼ or 50 per cent. more.

Hair Nets.

	Each.	Per doz.
No. 21410. Invisible Hair Nets of double hair, for front only	$0.05	$0.55
No. 17698. Hair Nets, silk, all colors, and gray, for back hair	.08	.85
No. 17696. Hair Nets, all colors, for back hair	.10	1.00
No. 17691. Hair Nets, Gerster, coarse, hand made, for back hair	.15	1.40

Ladies' Wigs.

No. 21411. These wigs are all ventilated on a delicate open mesh foundation. They are perfect in fit, having a graceful and natural appearance not found in wigs of other manufacture.

	Each.
Short hair, cotton foundation	$10.00
Short hair, silk foundation	12.00
Hair, 18 inches long	15.00
Hair, 24 inches long	18.00

This is only for ordinary shades; light and half gray are worth 25 per cent. more; if very gray, 50 per cent. more.

Full Beards.

No. 21412. On wire		$1.00
No. 21413. Ventilated		2.00

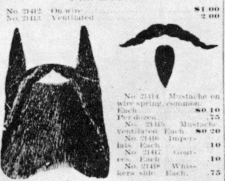

No. 21414. Mustache on wire spring, common.
Each $0.10
Per dozen .... .75
No. 21415. Mustache, ventilated. Each ...$0.20
No. 21416. Imperials. Each .... .10
No. 21417. Goatees. Each .... .10
No. 21418. Whiskers, side. Each .... .75

The above come in dark and medium shades only.

Men's Wigs.

Directions for measuring the head for a wig, to insure a good fit, and mention number of inches.

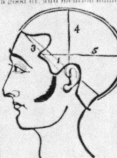

No. 1. The circumference of the head.
No. 2. Forehead to nape of the neck.
No. 3. Ear to ear, across the forehead.
No. 4. Ear to ear, over the top.
No. 5. Temple to temple, around the back.

TO MEASURE FOR A TOUPEE.

Cut a piece of paper the exact size and shape of the bald spot, also the measure around the head, and mention which side the parting is on.

No. 21419. Men's Toupee, weft foundation. Price, each $5.50
No. 21420. Men's Toupee, ventilated foundation. Price, each $10.00
No. 21421. Toupee paste, for keeping the same in place. Per stick $0.50
No. 21422. Men's Full Wigs, for street wear, weft seam with crown cotton foundation. Price, each $8.00
No. 21423. Men's Wigs, silk foundation, vegetable net seam. Price, each $12.00
No. 21424. Men's Wigs, silk foundation, gauze net seam. Price, each $15.00
No. 21425. Men's Wigs, silk foundation, hair lace. Price, each $21.00
Extra shades will be charged according to color.

Central Village, Conn., Dec. 29, 1896.
Sears, Roebuck & Co.: Dear Sirs: We received the goods all right and are very much pleased with them. They all fitted correctly. Everybody is pleased with them and thought they were cheap.
Yours respectfully, ELMER M. RIDER.

Will Send Other Orders.

Milford Center, O., Jan. 2, 1896.
Sears, Roebuck & Co.: I received the clothes to-day and must say I was surprised. I am well pleased and will favor you with another order soon.
Yours respectfully. JAMES POWERS.

They All Write Us This Way.

Jacksonville, Ark., Jan. 2, 1897.
Sears, Roebuck & Co.: My husband received suit and cape in good order, for which please accept our thanks. Highly pleased with suit. As to the cape I hardly know how to express myself. I am so pleased. I compared it with a $10 cape; it was far superior to any. Am highly pleased to say the least. My husband has induced his friend, Bro. James P. Hatfield, to order a suit of you. Perhaps you have received his order ere this. Please send me samples of dress ginghams and prints, also price list of same. Again thanking you, I remain, respectfully yours,
MRS. ADA HEARD.

Men's, Ladies' and Children's Hosiery.

In this department we are especially well stocked. We have everything desirable for infants, all sizes and qualities for children. Hosiery for slim ladies, plump ladies and for fleshy ladies, regular lengths or opera lengths. Men's half hose in all qualities of cotton or wool. Our ladies', men's or children's hosiery, called fast black, are positively fast black and will not fade in washing or crock and become gray in wearing. We have cotton hosiery from 5 cents a pair and upwards; Lisle thread hosiery, 25 cents per pair; silk hosiery, 50 cents to $3.00 per pair; also a large variety of fancy hosiery in all the newest Paris novelties, opera or ordinary lengths.

Our liberal terms offer applies in this department. Any goods will be sent by express C.O.D., subject to examination on receipt of $1.00, balance and express charges payable at express office. 3 per cent. discount for cash in full with order.

These goods can be sent by mail when you send enough extra to pay postage.

Average weight of cotton hose, 30 ounces to the dozen; 2½ ounces per pair; wool, 3½ ounces per pair.

Ladies' Fancy Hosiery.

No. 21426. Pin striped, which is very neat and popular. Per pair $0.05
Per dozen .... .55
No. 21427. Ladies' Fine 20 Gauge Cotton Hose, extra long, elastic hemmed tops, in a great variety of striped colors, with black boot pattern. Per pair $0.08
Per dozen .... .90
No. 21428. Ladies' Fast Black Boot pattern, with fancy colored tops, also in fancy stripe tops, pretty new effects, full seamless foot, elastic hemmed top. Per pair $0.12½
Per dozen 1.40

Special Drives at 19 Cents Per Pair.

No. 21429.

No. 21429. Ladies' Fancy Hose, with black boot pattern, white tipped heel and toe, full regular made, very good weight, high spliced heel and toe. Either plain or fancy ribbed leg, fancy light colors, such as blue and pink. Plain and not ribbed, come in fancy stripes, red and white, nile and white, blue and white. These goods are very fashionable and have a great demand this season; in retail stores at 35 cents.
Our price, per pair $0.19
Per dozen 2.10

Ladies' Fancy Boot Patterns at 25 Cents Per Pair.

No. 21430. Fast Black Boot Pattern, white tipped heel and toe, extra fine gauge, full fashioned, double heel and toes, fancy tops in plain light colors, pink, blue, yellow and heliotrope.
Per pair $0.25
Put up in boxes, six pair assorted colors in a box, for $1.40

No. 21430

No. 21431. Fast Black Boot Pattern, colored tops with fancy made ribbed leg, full regular made and handsomely finished, double heeled and toed, which are white tipped; come in the following shades. Pink, pale blue, yellow, nile, heliotrope and red, having a group of three black stripes about an inch apart, and making a very pretty stocking, which, to all appearances and wear, are as good as Lisle thread. Per pair $0.25
Put up in boxes of six pairs of assorted colors, per box 1.40

No. 21431

DIED OF VIBRATION.

SMEAR AD—1874 STYLE. *The wars of competing farm machinery manufacturers in the seventies were savage. This smear ad "proved" that the 1865 apron-type thresher brought prosperity to Farmer Jones (No. 1), while the 1874 vibrator-type of Farmer Gotsold (No. 2) brought the Sheriff (No. 3), and ruin.*

THERE'S ALWAYS AN AD MAN. *This purported to be simply a "Moonlight Scene in the Far West," but the moon and the locomotive headlamp just happen to reveal that the train is loaded with J. I. Case machines.*

AUCTION!

Saturday, May 18, 10 o'clock, A. M.

Will be sold at Public Auction, at the present residence of R. B. KELLOGG, in Windsor, the following described property, consisting of

HOUSEHOLD FURNITURE, and Farming Tools.

One Bureau, one Sofa,
  Lot of Mirrors and Chairs,
Dining tables, Center tables,
  And pictures in pairs.

One nice Stewart stove
  Which cannot be beat,
For a family to use
  To cook what they eat.

And several other Stoves,
  And pipe in connection,
Which you can't tell from new
  But by close inspection.

All the things in the pantry,
  Tin pans, jars and jugs,
Tin pails, plates and platters,
  And white earthern mugs.

Demijohns, butter firkins,
  Bail boxes and trays,
Which you know to be used
  In a great many ways.

One barrel of Cider,
  And empty barrels, too
Four kegs, a lot of bottles,
  We shall offer to you.

One barrel of pork
  We shall sell on that day,
And some one will buy it,
  But who, we can't say.

One wheelbarrow, three axes,
  Two wood-saws, three hoes,
One spade fork, two shovels,
  And manure fork, goes.

Two hay-cutters, two forks,
  One feed-box that's pine,
One express sleigh, four halters
  And flour barrels, nine.

Five harnesses, two robes,
  And straps without number,
One Mexican saddle, 2 bridles,
  And a small pile of lumber.

Two bitting bridles, two martingales,
  Open headstalls, three,
Six surcingles, three blankets,
  I want you to see.

Two monkey wrenches, one crow-bar,
  One refrigerator new,
One nice sleigh-pole & fixtures
  I'm keeping for you.

To one two-horse wagon
  I now call your attention,
And a great many things
  I don't think to mention.

ow come one and all,
  That I may be blest
With a call from my friends
Before I go West.

R. B. KELLOGG.
A. B. BURKE, Auct.

Windsor, Vt. May 10, 1867.

Of Feasts and Fairs and

Get-Togethers

ONE OF our great myths is that farmers are dour, loathing merriment as the work of Satan. Nothing could be further from the truth. From the very first, farm communities have had their own group pleasures. Perhaps the ones that were anticipated with most excitement were the county fair and, for the childrn at least, the circus.

After the railroad came, the circus was an annual event, and in every community one or more barns were plastered in advance with huge gaudy posters exaggerating what in truth was quite a show anyway. ("Hurry, hurry, hurry!") The kids on these farms got free tickets to the main tent, and the side-show, too. ("He's alive! He bites off the heads . . .") Far more important than the biggest circus, however, was the smallest county fair. Held near the county seat, it ran three days, and to it went the farmer and all his family, the women bringing canned fruits and quilts and needlework for competitive display and possibly a "premium." The men entered sleek teams of horses, fat oxen and pigs, and perhaps an arrogant bull; and also astounding pumpkins, ears of corn, head-high wheat on the stalk, so that the be-ribboned judges should see what Sims Hill or Stratford Hollow had to brag about. There was horse-racing, too. And this was the time to beware the shell-game operators who came with the slicker carnival. The fairs, both state and county, were planned to follow harvest, when late autumn haze was on the hills. The fair has a long history in America. It dates back to 1810, when Farmer Elkanah Watson of Berkshire County, Massachusetts, staged a little cattle show.

ANNUAL FAIR

Belknap Agricultural Association. $2,500.00 in Premiums.

THIRTEENTH ANNUAL FAIR
TO BE HELD AT

Laconia, N. H., Sept. 3, 4 and 5, '89

And Continuing the 6th if Previously Interrupted by a Storm.

——Special Attractions Every Day.——

WEDNESDAY, Sept. 4, will be known as Governor's Day, at which time distinguished gentlemen will be present.

THURSDAY, Sept. 5, will be the Grand Belknap Carnival Day, at which time it is proposed to surpass any previous closing day in the magnitude of amusements.

Large Display of Blooded Stock. **Trotting and Running Races Each Day.**

Good Music by Brass Bands. Exhibits will be Free, and Passengers Half Rates on Railroad.

Sam Hodgson, President. J. Frank Crockett, Vice-President. Orran W. Tibbetts, Treas. True E. Prescott, Sec'y.

The county fair usually came right after the end of haying. Scores of them were held from Maine to Oregon.

The circus comes to town in Newton, New Jersey.

PROTOTYPE OF THE PARKING LOT. *Horses and wagons at a Grange picnic in New Jersey.*

Crowds at the Fair in Gay's Mills, Wisconsin, 1907.

The farmers planned far ahead for their own exhibits and had great interest in what their neighbors had to show.

The attractions ranged from a wood-sawyers' tournament, such as the one above at Lafayette, Indiana, to an auto parade, such as the one at the Pratt County Fair in Kansas.

And of course the sideshows, always the most ree-markable
on the face of the earth.

The medicine man, an American institution, selling an Indian "sure cure."

New Jersey Grangers going home from the fair.

VERY OFTEN pleasure was combined with getting a task done. Out of this came all the "bees." Possibly the husking-bee, with a red ear worth a kiss, and winding up with a dance on the old barn floor, became the best known. There were box-socials, too, and pound-parties to which everybody brought a pound of butter, or cheese, or cake—or its equivalent—for support of the minister, whose services each Sunday were both a social and a spiritual get-together. There were quilting-bees, apple-paring-bees, barn-raisings, sugarings-off, and of course weddings, and a shiveree (charivari) to serenade the newly married couple. The Glorious Fourth was an opportune time to gather, often for a picnic beside a lake or stream. Town meeting in New England, and Election Day everywhere, were not only reason enough to gather but a civic obligation.

The main object of all bees was to help a neighbor, as in this party devoted to dressing flax, called scutching.

DOWN AT THE HUSKING BEE. *Eastman Johnson's painting of Cornhusking at Nantucket, now in New York's Metropolitan Museum, has become a classic. The photograph below, though obviously posed, shows what appears to be a genuine cornhusking bee down in the old barn, with plenty of red ears being uncovered (top), each good for a kiss from one's best girl.*

SQUARE DANCE. *After the husks were pushed aside, the fiddle and banjo struck up* Money Musk, *and all hands balanced partners.*

THE APPLE BEE. *A century ago apple pie was, as it is today, the favorite American dessert and a breakfast dish in New England. This festive group has gathered to peel and slice apples, string them on cords, and then hang from the kitchen ceiling until dry. Drying apples gave the entire house a pleasant fruity smell and dried-apple pies filled in the gap between the fresh-apple seasons.*

The womenfolk liked to gather for almost any kind of a "bee," like this quilting party in Virginia.

Almost every town had its band, fife-and-drum corps or some such group to
provide the music for Fourth of July picnics, parades, important occasions
and holiday celebrations.

The parlor of the farm home was commonly used only for special occasions and for music. More often than not, the music came from an organ like those made in Vermont by the famous Estey Company, which were to be found everywhere on the farm frontier. Sometimes there'd be a musical evening. Cousin Lottie would bring her guitar and all would gather round the organ or the piano to play and sing the old songs and learn the new ones.

MOVING DAY. *When a family had to move, the neighbors rallied round, brought their teams and buckboards to help out, and made a picnic out of a chore.*

VOLUNTEER FIRE DEPARTMENT. *The fire department was a kind of club, and the volunteers, proud of their horses and engine, would devote hours and hours to them.*

GONE FISHIN'. *There were many pleasures a man could enjoy by himself.*

RURAL DOODLING. *All rural characters were generally supposed to be addicted to whittling, a belief that no doubt promoted this excellent turn-of-the-century photograph.*

TROTTING AND PACING. *Save when seasonal work pressed too hard, a man could always take time off to train and exercise his fast trotter, who might not be a champion like Jay Eye See, but might win a race at the fair.*

JAY EYE SEE.
RECORD 2:10.

RACING. *The sport was not only in the race itself but in the planning, the boasts, the secret information, the arguments and the wagers.*

The city slicker, with all his fine equipment— and no game—fails to impress the farmer.

The coon hunts, fabled in story, also helped the farmer remove an enemy of his chickens.

Every settler owned a gun and most prided themselves on their marksmanship. These sharpshooters in George Caleb Bingham's painting of 1854 are engrossed in running up scores for the prize—in this case a beef critter. Turkey shoots, like the one below, were not uncommon. The bird was tied down and the contestants took turns firing at it or its replacement.

He *"knew hogs" and was quick to enter a weight-guessing contest.*

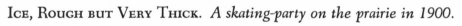

ICE, ROUGH BUT VERY THICK. *A skating-party on the prairie in 1900.*

Sugaring Off

THE SUGARING-OFF was an annual event in all communities blessed with rock-maple trees. It was the climax of the brief season when days were warm, nights frosty, and sap ran in rivers from the spouts driven into each tree. The sap was gathered daily, taken to the sugar-house and boiled, either in a big kettle over an open fire, or in a long evaporator pan set on a brick furnace. Fifty gallons of sap made a gallon of golden syrup. To make hard sugar the farmer moved the syrup to a sugaring-off pan, there to simmer until ready. It was then that neighbors came for the sugaring-off. Each guest had his eating-tools—a wooden paddle which he dipped into the thickening syrup, a smaller paddle used as a spoon to eat with. (City visitors who found the paddles as difficult as chopsticks were given spoon and saucer.) For dessert, pans of hard-packed snow were brought in, hot syrup dribbled over them, and the guest deftly rolled the sweet ribbons on his small paddle or fork. To offset the rich fare, a tub of the sourest pickles ever made stood handy. Everything was free, all hands ate their fill, the kids romped, songs were sung, and the experts commented, like so many wine tasters, on the quality of the season. Meanwhile, the farmer filled wooden buckets or tin pails with what, in many a community, might well be the most valuable crop of the year.

The Grange was one of the great influences in bringing farm people together and in giving them political direction. The hero of the Western Grangers was William Jennings Bryan, the Boy Orator of the Platte; and their heroine was Mary Elizabeth Lease. ("What you farmers need is to raise less corn and more hell!" she told them when the ten-cent corn was a drug on the market.) "I Pay for All" was the great slogan that expressed the farmer's conviction that he was the foundation of the nation, the keystone of the economy.

A meeting of the Grangers in Scott County, Illinois, 1873.

POLITICS ON THE FRONTIER. *Elections were serious business and farmers listened carefully to what the candidates had to say. This is the way stump-speaking in 1854 appeared to George Caleb Bingham, whose genre paintings focused on farmers and backwoodsmen in mid-century Missouri.*

A majority of farm people were devout enough to drive many miles in all weather to meeting.

Whether or not he had business there, Court Day was a good excuse for a man to visit the county seat. Its bulletin board was filled with notices, official and otherwise, warnings, reward posters, advertisements and announcements.

The tents of Chautauqua, presenting lecturers, etc., etc., dotted the whole country, bringing entertainment and perhaps culture to farm and village.

Volume XI.] SAN FRANCISCO, SATURDAY, MAY 6, 1876. [Number 19.

The agricultural press, including scores of weekly or monthly papers such as the Rural New Yorker *and the* Prairie Farmer *had a large audience among progressive farmers.*

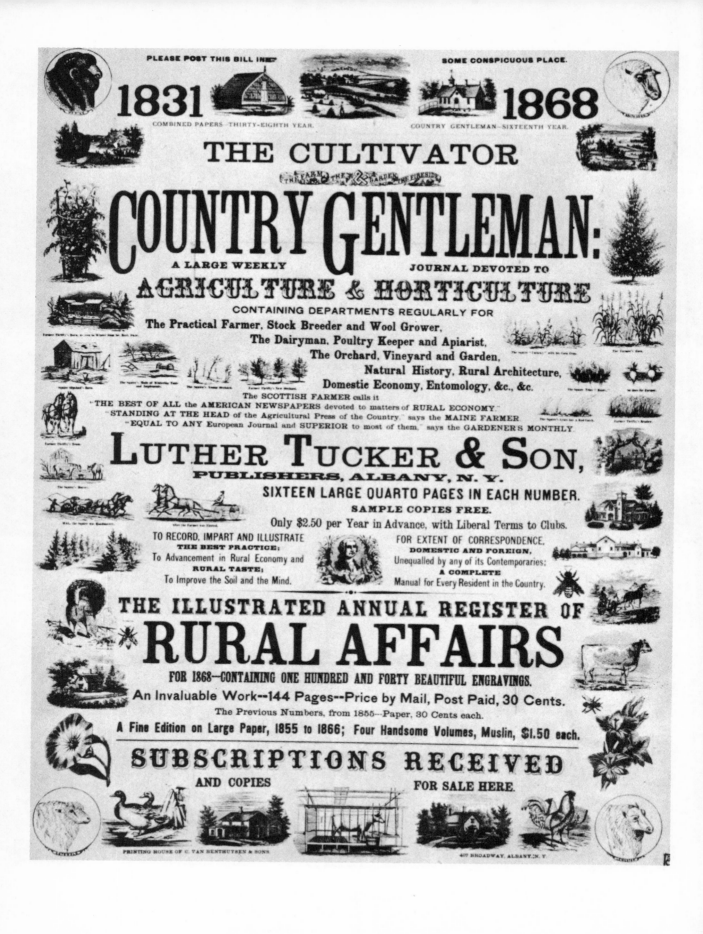

182

Thanksgiving

THE REALLY great event in early American farm life, however, came when the pumpkins were golden . . .

Thanksgiving was the farmer's traditional festival long before President Lincoln proclaimed it a national holiday. It stemmed from Plymouth where the devout colonists wished to praise God for the bounty of a fruitful harvest in their land of New Canaan on Massachusetts Bay. The Pilgrims were essentially farmers. Three centuries later, Thanksgiving belongs to all of us, though it is considered particularly fitted to the farm.

The romantic aspects of the First Thanksgiving Day have perhaps never been more idyllically shown than in this painting by Jennie Brownscombe (1850-1936), American artist, which hangs in Pilgrim Hall at Plymouth, Massachusetts, and shows New England's pioneer settlers giving thanks for their harvest of 1621.

Thanksgiving is near.

Grandmother bastes and browns the noble big
bird in the kitchen range . . .

Grandfather does his duty.

. . . and the climax of the year—Thanksgiving dinner.

Picture Credits

The numbers refer to pages. "T" is top; "B" is bottom; "L" is left; "R" is right; "C" is center.

Bettmann Archive—20 B, 166 T

Bostwick Studio—22 B, 35 TL, 35 TR, 42 TL, 51 T, 51 B, 52 B, 54 B, 62, 71, 75 B, 77 TL, 77 TR, 78 TL, 78 TR, 79 T, 80 BL, 87, 101 T, 101 B, 124 T, 127, 131 T, 137 B, 138 T, 141, 144 BL, 170 T, 181 T, 184 T

Brown Brothers—21 T, 23 T, 23 B, 25, 26 B, 27 T, 27 BR, 28 TL, 28 TR, 29 T, 30 T, 30 B, 40 T, 40 CR, 42 TR, 42 B, 43, 49 B, 50 T, 53 T, 56 T, 60 T, 60 B, 61 T, 61 B, 64 T, 64 CL, 64 CR, 65 T, 68 T, 69 TR, 72 B, 75 T, 77 BL, 77 BR, 89 TL, 89 B, 90 B, 93 T, 93 B, 94 TL, 106 T, 110 B, 111 B, 117 T, 117 B, 118 T, 118 B, 120 T, 120 B, 121 T, 121 B, 122 T, 122 B, 129, 130 B, 131 B, 132 B, 133, 134 BL, 135 T, 135 B, 138 B, 139 T, 139 B, 140 T, 140 B, 144 T, 145, 158 T, 158 B, 161 T, 161 B, 162 T, 162 B, 164 B, 165, 168 T, 169 B, 172 T, 173 T, 173 B, 175, 178 T, 183, 184 BL, 184 BR, 185

J. I. Case Company—154 T, 154 B, 171 B

Chicago, Burlington & Quincy Railroad—19 B, 40 CL, 89 TR, 94 B, 130 T, 150 TL, 150 TR, 167 B

Jesse Ebert—36, 37

Fort Worth Art Center—26 T

Newell Green—17, 47 T, 123 B

Irma G. Haselwood—title page

Grant Heilman—15, 16 T, 16 B, 22 T, 29 B, 88, 91 T, 96 TL

F. Hal Higgins—57 T, 96 B, 100 T, 104 TR, 104 CR, 104 B, 105 BL, 105 BR, 106 B, 107 T, 107 B, 112 T, 112 B, 113, 115 T, 124 B, 181 B

Mrs. Myra Holbrook—31, 54 T, 90 T, 132 T

Illinois Central Railroad—33

Library of Congress—18 B, 19 T, 27 BL, 34 B, 35 B, 47 B, 53 B, 55 T, 55 B, 63 B, 65 B, 66 T, 68 B, 69 TL, 72 TL, 72 TR, 78 B, 92 T, 115 B, 123 C, 125 T, 125 B, 126 B, 149 T, 159 T, 159 B, 160 T, 160 B, 166 B, 172 BL, 172 BR, 174 T, 178 B, 179, 180

Metropolitan Museum of Art—164 T

The National Archives—79 B, 170 B

Nebraska State Historical Society—20 T, 34 B, 39 T, 66 B, 99 T, 126 T, 167 T, 174 B

The Newark Museum—143

New York State Historical Association—18 T, 50 B, 76 T, 85, 98 T, 136 T, 136 B, 137 T, 144 BR, 156 B

New-York Historical Society—21 B, 94 TR, 96 TR, 97, 122 C, 146, 147, 148 T, 148 B, 149 B, 155 T, 157, 182

New York Public Library—44, 45, 52 T, 82, 83, 84, 103, 119 T, 134 T, 134 BR, 151, 152, 153, 171 T

Northern Pacific Railway—28 B, 64 B

Ohio State Archaeological and Historical Society—19 B, 69 B, 169 T

Oregon Historical Society—67, 100 B, 108, 109 T

Smithsonian Institution—163

Underwood & Underwood—40 B, 56 B, 76 B, 80 BR, 91 B, 92 B, 99 B, 116 B

U. S. Department of Agriculture—57 B, 58 T, 58 B, 59 T, 59 B, 70, 81 T, 81 B, 98 B, 109 B

Vermont Development Commission—24, 123 T

State Historical Society of Wisconsin—38 T, 38 B, 41, 48 T, 48 B, 73, 80 T, 110 T, 111 T, 116 T, 150 B